THE AMAZING MRS LIVESEY

The remarkable story of Australia's greatest imposter

FREDA MARNIE NICHOLLS

ALLEN&UNWIN
SYDNEY · MELBOURNE · AUCKLAND · LONDON

First published in 2016

Allen & Unwin
83 Alexander Street
Crows Nest NSW 2065
Australia
Phone: (61 2) 8425 0100
Email: info@allenandunwin.com
Web: www.allenandunwin.com

Cataloguing-in-Publication details are available
from the National Library of Australia
www.trove.nla.gov.au

ISBN 978 1 76029 014 6

Internal design by Lisa White
Set in 12.5/18 pt Minion by Midland Typesetters, Australia
Printed and bound in Australia by Griffin Press

10 9 8 7 6 5 4 3 2

Dedicated to Frank George Bolan

CONTENTS

PROLOGUE

My name is Luita Aichinger, and I am the granddaughter of Florence Elizabeth Ethel Livesey, or 'The Amazing Mrs Livesey' as she became known in newspapers in the 1940s and 1950s.

Unfortunately I never met my grandmother, but I feel I have a reasonably good insight into her life, as my father, Frank, left me a number of precious audiotapes, describing his journey throughout these years, with and without her. It was a journey of heartache, sorrow and an unlikely upbringing.

My father passed away in 2005, at the age of 82. He always said he would not have traded his life for quids, and lived by the saying 'Don't Fence Me In', a song we played at his funeral at his request. We had many talks around the kitchen table over the years, him sitting there with a cigarette in one hand and a beer in the other, telling me about his younger years and his younger brother, Basil. My father's chats always intrigued me.

My father lost contact with his brother Basil. It was only about ten years before my father died that they found each other again, two old men by then—how sad, I thought, that these two brothers had lost so much of their time together. My father had a tough exterior, but beneath it all was a man who had felt hurt and rejected by a mother who was absent from his life at a time when a young boy was in need of a mother's love.

Dad led an adventurous life, with my mother by his side and eight children at foot, me being number five. He managed to teach himself the art of signwriting, and passed down his trade to three of my brothers and his grandsons, who to this day are still signwriters. My father told me I had a beautiful hand, and persuaded me to take up this art, and at nineteen I came second in the state as an accomplished ticketwriter.

For many years my father held an understandable degree of bitterness towards his mother Ethel, stating he never wanted to see her again. But, years later he needed to find his birth certificate to find out more about himself, something he tried to do right up until he died. Sadly, his death certificate is only half complete; his birth details were unknown.

My sister June and I first became interested in finding out more about our family after June visited a dentist over eighteen years ago. He told June she had particularly dark gums and asked about her family history, but she had no answer to give him on our father's side. So she started to delve a little deeper into dad's past, writing to the Department for Child Welfare in South Australia.

My own research into my grandmother's activities started not long after, when the Child Welfare Department replied to June's letter. An astonishingly large amount of paperwork followed, which June handed over to me.

In 2011, my research took me to the State Library of New South Wales, where I punched my grandmother's name into their search engine, and spent most of the day printing out a trail of newspaper clippings, all on the 'Amazing Mrs Livesey'. I was absolutely astounded, and excited, to finally start putting some answers together. My daughter Jessica also found a video of my grandmother speaking of her innocence on a British Pathé newsreel. I was so excited to hear her speak—this was my father's mother, at last.

In 2013, when I caught up with an old friend, author Freda Nicholls, I told her what I'd learnt about my grandmother, and mentioned that we still couldn't find my father's birth certificate. Freda became as caught up as I was in researching this remarkable woman, and two long years later, she finally found dad's birth certificate, uncovering along the way many other incredible facts.

Ethel Livesey's crime sheet is hard to defend, given the number of cases made against her, and an unbelievable list of aliases she invented for herself over a 30-year period. But this all has to be taken into context. The world in the 1930s was in the midst of a global Depression, and many people, including my grandmother, resorted to desperate measures in order to make ends meet. Being a single mother with two young boys would have compounded this. My grandmother made some bad choices in men throughout her life, and I can't justify her leaving her children while she lived the high life, but I was not in her shoes at the time, so I cannot judge.

Her life seemed to be one that was deceitful, as she fed off other people's generosity and trustfulness. How could anyone do this and have a conscience? I will never know the answer.

Our family line continues in Australia through her two sons and their descendants, and I am grateful that I had a father who loved and cared for all of his children, and for the life and adventures he gave us. Thankfully the saying 'The apples don't fall far from the tree' didn't apply here.

Luita Aichinger

My mother was quite a woman.

The day after Ethel got out of going to gaol, she sat us down, my brother Basil and me, and told us a few things. She would have been in her late forties about then, and was looking knackered after months of scrutiny by the cops, the media and the courts.

Over a couple of hot, dry, stifling summer days in 1946, we sat in my brother's house in Adelaide while his wife fussed over us; both Basil and me had plenty of questions for our mother. She told us her version of events, trying to justify herself I reckon, but you never knew whether to believe her or not. She never let the truth get in the way of a good story.

Years later I decided to do a bit of digging, not like you can on computers like now. I wrote letters, lots of letters. I had to find out about my family, and I needed to find my birth certificate. I found all sorts of weird and wonderful things about her instead, facts she wouldn't have been able to dispute even if she was still here.

This is her story.

1

MISS SWINDELLS

Florence Elizabeth Ethel Swindells was born in Manchester on 24 September 1897, that much is true.

The Swindells were originally farmers from Lancashire, but it was two brothers, Francis and Martin, who in the early 1800s branched out into milling cotton. They must have been a game lot, and tough. The family story goes that Francis ran away from home and his very strict father when he was about sixteen. He made it down to London and went into service, as they called it back then, as a groom to a gentleman.

Late one night Francis was sitting up next to the coachman taking his master's family home over Hounslow Heath, a hangout of bandits and footpads (robbers on foot), when two highwaymen bailed them up.

Francis grabbed the reins from the terrified coachman, ducking the highwaymen's fire, and drove the horses furiously through the night, eventually getting the relieved family safely back home. His master rewarded him with a wad of cash, and not long afterwards he married his sweetheart Mary, a servant in the same household. They moved up to Manchester to raise a family, where his brother Martin joined them.

Manchester back then was known as 'Cottonopolis', on account of its massive textile industry, and Francis and Martin got in on the act, building seven large cotton mills over the years. By the time they were middle aged they were extremely well off, and at the height of the Industrial Revolution even bought and restored a 16th-century three-storey manor house.

It wasn't from these Swindells that Ethel was apparently descended. Rather, Francis and his brother Martin supposedly had an illegitimate cousin James—who they employed as a cotton spinner, and then a cotton buyer. He must have been pretty good at it because the job was handed down to his son, and then his grandson, Frank Swindells—Ethel's father. Frank's family never owned a mill, but he was certainly involved with the business and held plenty of coin, just not in the same league as Francis and Martin's families.

The Swindells brothers were apparently good-looking as well as rich. When they built Clough Mill, their first cotton mill, the local papers said they were two of the finest-looking men to ever come to the town, but maybe that was the money talking. The press often remarked on the striking good looks and engaging personalities of the Swindells family, something that was certainly carried down to Ethel.

Tall for a girl back then, standing nearly five foot seven, Ethel had long brown hair and big blue eyes that held your attention even when you didn't want them to. Her mother Elizabeth was a stickler for manners and made sure Ethel spoke the Queen's English, rather than picking up the broad accent of the town, and she always insisted her girls were well 'turned out', looking their best. Ethel always loved to look her best, wearing the most expensive clothes and jewellery she could get her hands on.

She was the only child in her family for eleven years, until her little sister Mabel came along. Her father had always doted on her, and she adored him, but suddenly she was no longer the centre of attention, and had to share his affection. How could she be her father's special girl when there was another?

Her father would often take her to the theatre, opera and vaudeville shows in the busy Manchester town centre, to get her out of her mother's hair, and Ethel loved the excitement, the fantasy. But it was the first silent film she remembered seeing at the Oxford Picture House on a cold winter's evening in 1911 that she would talk about the most. Watching that short black-and-white film on Captain Scott's expedition to the South Pole, she was spellbound, taken into a whole other world. Her vivid imagination ran riot: that was *her* up there on screen with Scott, facing danger, triumphing over extremes, all to the accompaniment of loud, dramatic music pumped out on an upright piano.

As more movies were released and more picture houses opened, Ethel would sneak out whenever she could. A trip to the movies didn't come cheap, so she funded her trips with change she'd purloin from her father's pockets or mother's purse, but it was never enough. She learnt to sneak in, attaching herself to a group of people, often starting a casual conversation with one of them as they made their way into the theatre. That way she could often avoid the ticket collector and usher, sitting just separate from the group, alone in the dark, imagining herself up there with the main movie star.

Her parents sent Ethel to an exclusive girls' school, but she didn't focus much on her education. Instead she would egg her friends into all sorts of scrapes or take on dares—swimming the big water canals that ran beside the mills, or meeting boys from the nearby Manchester Grammar School. Anything for a bit of attention. Ethel completed the school work, but she was going to be a movie star up there on the big screen—she was going to have a life of adventure and live the high life, the papers would write about how much money she had, what clothes she wore and how fabulous she was; she would be famous.

It was probably about this time that Ethel learnt the power of a name. The Swindells held plenty of status and power in the town, and she took advantage of her surname to get what she wanted, or to get out of trouble.

And there was plenty of trouble ahead. It was 1914, and the fun-loving Ethel was turning seventeen.

2

MRS CARTER

Ethel was three months short of eighteen when she married Alexander 'Alec' Carter, against her father's wishes.

She lied about her age at the registry office, left school and home, and moved to the town of Eccles to the north of Manchester, where her new husband was working as a stationer with his father.

The Great War had started in August the previous year, and Ethel later recalled big parties in the street, and how the boys from the Manchester Grammar School talked of nothing else except fighting for King and Country, with large numbers of boys and men signing up. They thought the war would last no more than a few months—that it would all be over by Christmas—and they were keen to be a part of it. But after a few months, the reality of war began filtering back, together with the lists of dead and wounded. The Manchester Regiment, where most of the local boys had ended up, were pinned down by the Turks at Gallipoli, and then the lists of the dead appeared in the papers, and included names of boys Ethel knew. Some of the young men had married their sweethearts just weeks or even days before heading off to war, never to return.

Alec was five years older than Ethel. It isn't really clear how they met, or why Ethel married him. Perhaps she was after a sense of security, but then she always did seem to like older men.

Alec didn't immediately enlist, as he was classed 'unfit for active service' when he first applied to join up with his father at the beginning of the war. By 1916, however, men were falling like flies, and the War Office began calling up those who had been rejected at the start. They were also having trouble getting labour to build roads, unload ships and carry supplies around the Western Front, so a Labour Corps was established, and this was where they sent Alec. He was trained as a gunner, to operate and load the howitzer heavy field guns, and was then sent to the Western Front in June 1916, leaving Ethel, four months pregnant, with his family.

Alec's father was recruited a few months later, so Ethel was then left with her mother-in-law and sisters-in-law, Doris and Gladys. None of the Carter women liked her, and she didn't think much of them either. Gladys was the same age as Ethel, and Doris two years older, and both of the daughters went off each morning and worked in their father's shop with their mother, keeping the shop going, leaving the pregnant young Ethel at home alone.

Ethel, like her mother-in-law, received money—a pension from the Ministry of Pensions in the War Office—which could be accessed once a week at the post office via a 'ring paper'. From October 1914, ring papers were issued to the wives and children of soldiers and sailors sent off on active duty. The names of dependants were given to the War Office by each serviceman; a numbered ring paper was then issued to the dependant, with wives receiving a bit over six pounds a week. Instead of having to wait a month for money to survive on from the serviceman's wage, all they had to do was go to the nominated post office, hand over the numbered ring paper that showed their name, this was checked off an enormous ledger, the ring paper holder would then sign in that same ledger and receive the money.

But Ethel was bored and lonely. Stuck in Eccles, she kept herself amused by going to the shops and spending her husband's money—it kept her happy as her belly grew. Rather than hand the money to her mother-in-law to help with living expenses, Ethel spent all of it on clothes, shoes and going to the movies, which led to some pretty heated disagreements. So Ethel moved back into her father's home, where she wasn't questioned about her spending habits—her father even gave her more money to spend.

She did her best to ignore the fact there was a war on—but that wasn't to last long. In early November 1916 a letter arrived from the War Office: Alec was missing in action, presumed dead.

Ethel's world crumbled. Fearing the worst, her head filled with dramatic images of Alec's body left lying out on a battle-field; she took to her bed and refused to leave. Her mother tried to coax her to eat for the sake of the baby, but all Ethel could do was cry, falling into an exhausted sleep each night.

Frank Alexander Carter was born on 26 November 1916, but Ethel couldn't even look at her newborn baby. Her parents decided to take baby Frank away and care for him in another part of the house, thinking their daughter would recover and love her baby when she was better.

Instead, Ethel woke one night to the sound of her baby crying, got up, packed a few things, and quietly left her parents' home.

3

MRS TAYLOR

Ethel went out into the street, and walked. She didn't care which direction she went, she just walked in the cool air as briskly as she could. It felt good after being cooped up in her room all that time. At first light she slowed and pulled up at the first open café she came across, collapsed into a chair and ordered a cup of tea.

She had never felt so directionless. All her energy seemed to have gone; all she felt was sadness. She had lost her husband, she didn't want to go back to her parents and face her baby, and she certainly couldn't go to her in-laws.

She sat quietly with her hands around the cup of tea on the table, having to lift it to her mouth with both hands because they were shaking so badly. The tea revived her, but when she'd finished and pulled out her purse to pay, she realised she didn't have much money, and no way of getting any more until the post office opened. Then the realisation hit: her husband was dead—would she still get his pension?

Rising from the table, she straightened her coat and went to the counter to hand over the coins for her tea. The lady behind the counter looked as tired as she herself felt.

'Are you alright?' the lady asked.

Ethel looked towards her, and then started to sway. 'Yes,' she replied, trying to clear her throat, 'I, uh, I . . .' When she couldn't get the words out, the lady looked at her in genuine concern. 'No, no, I'm not,' Ethel corrected herself quietly, and the lady's tired eyes softened. 'My husband is dead. I don't, I don't know what to do.' She was holding back tears now. 'And I, I, don't have much money, I . . .' and the tears fell.

The woman came out from behind the counter and placed her arms around Ethel. 'There, there love,' she said, gently holding her. 'It'll be alright.' As she held Ethel and wiped away her tears with the edge of her stained apron, she said with a smile, 'Tell you what love, the tea's on me—you just get home and look after yourself, eh?'

Ethel nodded and looked down at the faded lino floor. 'Thank you,' she said quietly. She pulled back her shoulders and looked at the kind woman, 'Thank you.'

Going back out into the cool morning air, Ethel felt momentarily elated. The woman had given her the cup of tea for free, it hadn't cost her a penny. Her mood changed when she thought about her lack of cash. She still had money, but not much. Where was she going? What was she going to do? How could she get money to live on? In the early morning light she stood on the pavement and twirled the thin gold wedding band on her ring finger, unsure what to do. She heard a train in the distance and just headed towards the sound; trains had always been linked with fun and adventure ever since she was a little girl, when her parents would take her to Blackpool for a week's break each year. The sound drew her like a magnet.

The railway station was on the Manchester–Liverpool line. Using the same skills she had picked up when sneaking into movie theatres, she avoided buying a ticket by attaching herself to a group of three women and their combined brood of young children as they moved onto the train. The women sat down and fussed over their kids and Ethel sat a couple of seats away. But she found she couldn't look at the kids, and when one of the babies began grizzling and then started to cry, she got up and walked to the other end of the carriage and leant against the window, closing her eyes in exhaustion.

———•·•———

'Tickets!' The command woke her with a start. Ethel looked up to see a conductor entering from the front carriage. It took a moment for her to figure out where she was; her brain felt like it was filled with glue, slowing everything down.

Hearing the screech of the train's brakes being applied, Ethel grabbed her bag and made her way to the door. Out of the corner of her eye she saw the conductor punching one of the mothers' tickets and looking at her as he continued making his way down the carriage. She opened the door as the train slowed and halted, and stepped out into the cool air.

Standing on the platform for a moment, she watched as the train pull away. She felt herself sway, and felt hot despite the cool air, but knew she had to keep moving. She had to get away, from everything. She stumbled towards the raised walkway over the tracks. Each step was tough, the stairs felt so steep. Weak and out of breath, she stopped at the top of the stairs and steadied herself as she again felt herself sway.

'You right, love?' a voice asked. She looked up and saw a bloke in an army uniform leaning against the rail, watching her. 'Are you alright?' he asked her again; moving towards her as she half fell onto the railing.

The sight of the uniform, and the feeling of being unwell, made her want to cry. 'I, I . . . no I don't feel well,' she blurted.

He came up beside her and grabbed her as her knees buckled. 'Whoa there!' he laughed. 'Come on, there's a seat this way. Think you'd better sit down for a while.' He steered her off the walkway, then helped ease her down onto a bench.

Ethel looked down at the ground and thanked him. She couldn't help but feel his eyes roaming over her.

'What's your name?' he asked.

'Ethel,' she replied, 'Ethel . . . Smith.' She didn't know why she didn't give him her real name. This way just felt right.

'Pleased to meet you, Ethel. I'm Billy—Billy Taylor. You from around here?'

Ethel shook her head as tears escaped and fell to the ground.

'There, there, love. Come on—tell Billy what's wrong,' he said, gently gripping her hand.

Still looking down she stifled a sob, not trusting her voice. She looked up, but the sight of his uniform once again made her cry. 'My husband, my . . . he's dead,' was all she could get out before her head fell against his shoulder in sorrow.

Billy patted her shoulder and held her for a moment before she pulled herself away, took a deep breath and wiped the tears from her eyes.

He looked at her for a moment, then stood and pulled her to her feet. 'Come on Ethel, let's go get a drink. We could both do with one, there's a pub up the way.' He gave her a smile and she nodded her head in reply—maybe a drink would help. They walked slowly up the street, Ethel leaning on Billy, who hobbled along.

She suddenly stopped and looked down at his legs. 'You're hurt!' she said quietly.

'A bit. Getting better. I'm up at that convalescent camp, at Knowsley. Decided to go out for an explore, exercise this gammy leg of mine—and look what I found!' he grinned. 'Come on, let's get that drink,' he said, leading her up the road.

———··———

Ethel woke with a thumping head and dry mouth, the light through the window hurting her eyes.

'Good morning, Mrs Taylor.'

She looked over at Billy in surprise: he was leaning beside her on one elbow, grinning. 'Wh-at?' she asked him, taking in the room and the bed, in which the two of them were lying.

He laughed. 'Just kiddin', love, but that's what I told the landlady when I knew you couldn't go anywhere. You're Mrs Billy Taylor while you're here.'

Ethel looked around her—at the dirty curtains, the paint peeling off the ceiling. She had no idea where she was and she had to ask.

'The Black Horse Inn,' Billy stated. 'In Rainhill. You don't remember?'

She felt ill, and it wasn't just the fever. She looked up at Billy and slowly shook her head from side to side.

'Not surprised,' he replied, reaching across to push some damp hair from her face. He looked at her with concern. 'You do have a bit of a fever—I'll go downstairs and see if I can get us some food and drink, eh? That'll perk you up.'

She looked at him and nodded. As he climbed out of bed and started to dress back into his uniform, she scrutinised him carefully. Down his right leg was a series of big, red, raw scars, with smaller ones peppering his left leg.

Ethel closed her eyes. What had she done?

She heard the door close and tried to sit up, but a wave of nausea hit her; she pulled the duvet up around her head and felt herself shiver. She was in no state to go anywhere.

She must have nodded off, because she woke to the sound of a tray clattering.

'Sorry, didn't mean to wake you,' Billy said as he limped towards her.

She hadn't realised she was so thirsty. Reaching up to the glass of water on the tray, she grabbed it and unsteadily brought it to her mouth, took a gulp, and then another. Concentrating on drinking the water meant she didn't have to look at Billy.

He placed the tray down and sat on the bed beside her, stroking her arm. 'Better?' he asked. Ethel nodded in reply, still not wanting to look at him.

She leant back against the pillow and closed her eyes, but the bed seemed to sway beneath her and she quickly opened them again.

Billy was looking at her with such concern that she started to cry. He scooped her up and held her against his chest, gently rocking her backwards and forwards. Despite the nausea and dread, she liked being held close when everything seemed to be going so wrong.

She wasn't sure how many nights they stayed in that room, but after horror sweats on the first couple of days, she felt her strength starting to return. Billy wiped her fevered body down with a towel; fed her, held her, cared for her and helped her across the hallway to the bathroom whenever she asked. In between he held her close, kissed her and looked after her. She was dependent on him, but didn't care. He had swept her away from the pain of losing her husband, of leaving her baby.

———

On what was to be their last day at the Black Horse, they lay together on the bed and Billy turned to her.

'I have to go back,' he began, stroking her arm. 'I'm absent without leave. I need to go back,' he repeated, looking down at her arm. 'But I didn't want to leave you when you were so ill,' he added quietly.

Ethel looked at him expectantly—there were plans to make, things to organise.

But before she could reply, there was a knock at the door. They looked at each other in surprise, and then to the wooden door as it opened. When two policemen and the smirking manageress walked into the room, Ethel shrieked.

'You're both under arrest,' the older officer stated.

'What for?' Billy asked, sitting up.

'You're not married are you?' he stated, looking at them as Ethel tried to hide under the duvet. 'You're both under arrest for giving false information to a lodging-house keeper.'

4

MRS SMITH

It was the first time Ethel was to appear in a newspaper, and she was glad she hadn't given her real name—there'd be time to explain all of that to Billy later. She felt sure no one would recognise her as 'Ethel Smith' when that name was printed in the paper.

She and Billy were taken to the police lock-up at nearby Preston. Ethel complained to them of a fever, which she still had a touch of, so they packed her off to hospital, where she was admitted. Two days later she was discharged from hospital and told to appear at the Preston Petty Sessions. She thought about not going—there were no police around to make her—but she wanted to see Billy again. They hadn't even talked about what was going to happen next . . . maybe he could get a ring paper she could use.

Arriving at the courthouse, she went into the office. There, behind a big wooden counter, stood an elderly man carefully filling out a ledger. Several other people waited patiently on her side of the counter until the old clerk told them what to do and where to go. She leant against the wall as she waited, until the clerk looked up at her expectantly.

'My name is Ethel Smith—I, I had to come here,' she said uncertainly.

The clerk looked at her, then referred to the ledger in front of him.

'You're not a witness—you're a defendant!' he exclaimed. She looked back at him in surprise, not knowing what that meant. 'You're supposed to be out the back!' He looked at her sternly.

Ethel didn't know what she was supposed to do. 'Come with me,' he ordered, raising one section of the counter and beckoning for her to come through. 'Didn't they tell you?' he demanded before turning away. 'John? John, I got one for you,' he called out down the hallway that loomed behind them.

Another older man, the warden in charge of the lock-up came down the dark hall towards them, looking at them questioningly. He and the clerk had a brief conversation before the warden indicated with a gesture for Ethel to follow him. They weaved their way through the back of the building and down some stairs until they came to a row of cells near the basement.

Ethel didn't want to go into one of those!

'Please,' she began. The warden stopped and turned to look at her.

'Do, do I have to go into one of *those*? I mean, I came here of my own free will. And I haven't done anything wrong,' she implored. 'Please,' she tried once more, reaching out and touching the man's upper arm.

He looked her up and down—a nicely turned-out dame, dolled up and speaking nice. 'You can sit by the door,' he suggested. 'But don't go anywhere,' he warned. 'We're full anyway,' he mumbled as he went to sit at his desk, then busied himself filling out papers that Ethel assumed were for her. As she sat quietly by the door she could hear the murmurs and movements in the dark cells and shuddered—she couldn't imagine herself in one of them.

Before long, a policeman came down from the court. 'William Taylor and Ethel Smith,' he called out in a loud, almost bored, tone. She stood and turned to watch the warden walking down towards the cells.

Down the dark hallway she heard the clunk of a key turning in its lock, followed by a shuffle of feet—then Billy came around the corner towards her. He looked older and seemed to limp more than she remembered. Had it only been two days since she last saw him? She wanted to go towards him, but the presence of the warden and policeman, and the warning look Billy gave her, held her back.

'You haven't got a lawyer?' the policeman asked. Ethel looked at him blankly and Billy shook his head. 'You don't need one. Just state your case to the magistrate,' he said gruffly to them both. 'Follow me,' he ordered, then headed up the stairs with his two defendants in tow.

Ethel kept trying to catch Billy's eye, but he refused to look at her. The warden followed close behind, herding them into the court.

Those assembled inside the court looked at them with open curiosity as the policeman motioned towards the defendant's box and told them to take a seat. Ethel scanned the scattered faces before her, surprised by the animosity behind one woman's hateful gaze.

They had barely sat down when a door opened and the court clerk called out, 'All rise!' With a shuffle of feet the court rose almost as one, then watched as an elderly man dressed in a dark cloak entered and seated himself on what appeared to be a wooden throne in the middle of a raised box. He looked down at the court as the lawyers and the gallery followed his lead and sat down. Ethel was fascinated.

The clerk stood with a piece of paper in front of him. 'Private William Taylor and Miss Ethel Smith, you are charged under the Aliens Restriction Order for giving false information to a lodging-house keeper where you resided as a married couple.'

The magistrate looked at them, before asking in an almost bored tone, 'How do the defendants plead?'

Billy stood and said, 'Not guilty!' The magistrate frowned at him.

Ethel noticed the clerk motioning for her to stand, which she quickly did, loudly stating, 'Not guilty!'

'Do you have anything to say for yourselves? Private Taylor?' the magistrate turned first to Billy.

Billy stood in the defendant's box, not looking at Ethel but towards the assembled audience, watching one woman slowly weeping—the same woman who had looked at Ethel with such venom minutes before.

'Your Honour,' he began tentatively, 'I'm just back from the Front, where I've been with the King's Own Royal Regiment since the start of the war. I've been in Salonika and France, and was wounded two months back. Almost lost my leg. What I did was wrong, I shouldn't have been absent without leave, but this girl was ill and I was looking after her. It was just a moment of weakness.'

'Hardly a moment, Private Taylor, from what I have here,' the magistrate said, looking down at his notes. 'It was close to a week!' he added, to the amusement of those watching on.

'I couldn't leave her,' Billy responded, 'she was sick!' The magistrate raised his eyebrows.

'She's not *Miss* Smith either—she's a *Mrs*,' Billy stated, prompting murmurings in the small crowd, which was beginning to enjoy the drama.

'The fact is, if I am not mistaken, Private, that you are also married . . .'—Ethel, hearing herself gasp, looked at Billy—'to someone else,' the magistrate continued. 'And I understand there are children?'

'Yes, Your Honour—three,' he replied meekly.

Ethel felt her face warm as she looked at him. Married? Children?

'Be seated, Private Taylor,' the magistrate ordered.

'I'm sorry, Your Honour,' he muttered. 'I'm sorry,' he said looking towards his sobbing wife.

'Ethel Smith, do you have anything to say for yourself?' the magistrate asked as Billy sat heavily down beside her.

Ethel looked at her former lover in confusion as she tried to compose herself and answer the question, but Billy refused to return her look.

'Your Honour,' she started, rounding her vowels and distancing herself from Billy. 'Your Honour, I would like to state that this man took advantage of me!'

'Lying tart!' the wronged wife yelled at her, before collapsing into sobs.

The magistrate glared at the outspoken woman as Ethel tried to ignore the interruption. Her shock at hearing of the existence of Billy's family had now changed to anger, and she was going to let him have it.

'I was travelling by train to Liverpool to visit my dear, dear sister,' she began, imagining an emotive scene straight out of a movie, 'when I became ill and put myself off at the township of Rainhill. I was dizzy, sir, I had a fever and it came on me so suddenly,' she declaimed with great emotion, enjoying the effect her words were having on her audience. They were riveted, wanting to know more.

'I could hardly walk, Your Honour, and this man . . .' she said, looking down at Billy's hard face, '*this man* walked me to the Black Horse Inn, then plied me with alcohol until I was barely conscious.' There was some murmuring from the gallery. 'I was married, Your Honour, but my husband was killed recently on the Western Front, something I told this man when we met,' she stated loudly and clearly.

'I was sick, Your Honour—sick with grief. I was led away, filled with alcohol and I awoke the following morning in a bed, naked, with *him* beside me!' More gasps and murmurs from the crowd.

Ethel took a breath and felt tears of anger threatening—she let them flow.

'I could not leave the bed for days I was so ill.' She covered her face with her hands and gently sobbed for a moment. She looked up at the magistrate with tear-filled eyes. 'And I *certainly* did not know he was married and had children!' She realised a moment too late that perhaps she had no need to add that last statement if she was the wronged woman, but her words created angry murmuring from the gallery at the reminder of Billy's behaviour.

She looked at the magistrate as earnestly as she could, and implored in her proper English: 'I have been these last two days in hospital, sir. I came here today, still unwell, to defend myself and tell my story. I have been wronged, sir—I do not know how I will ever face my family again.'

With that she sat down, her face in her hands, and sobbed. Billy sat beside her dumbstruck.

'Thank you Miss, eh, Mrs Smith.' The magistrate cleared his throat, looking at the pair in the defendant's box. After what Ethel felt was a long time, he finally declared, 'As you are no doubt the victim in this case, Mrs Smith, and in such a precarious state of health, I find the charge against you proven, but I dismiss the charge against you. You are free to go.'

'Private William Taylor,' he said, turning his full attention to Billy. 'Your conduct has been nothing short of appalling, not worthy of someone serving in the King's Army. I sentence you to gaol for six months.'

Ethel left the courthouse as quickly as she could. She never even looked as poor Billy was led away, amid howls from his wife. She was elated and relieved that she was free to go, of course, but she was also still angry with Billy. How dare he treat her like that! She had thought that they might *be* together—that he would have given her a ring paper—but he obviously had no such intentions. She was angry with herself as well—she'd been foolish letting him use her like that. She vowed it would never happen again.

Ethel took her purse from her bag and sadly counted out the few coins it contained. Clicking the catch closed, she looked into her handbag and slowly pulled her husband's crumpled ring paper from the bottom. She read her name—Florence Elizabeth Ethel Carter—and thought of Alec. So much had happened in a short time. She thought of him lying some-where dead, his mangled body unclaimed. Then she thought of her baby, who she had never even held. She couldn't imagine bringing him up by herself—he was better off without her.

She crumpled up the ring paper and let it drop onto the pavement, then straightened her shoulders and strode off down the street.

5

MRS WARD

Barely two weeks later, on 30 December 1916, Ethel married again.

Florence Elizabeth Ethel Carter married Corporal Raymond 'Ray' Ward at the registry office in Old Flyde, just outside Blackpool.

Corporal Ward met the attractive war widow one night in the busy resort town of Blackpool, where he was enjoying a spell of rest and recreation leave. They were married the following day, just before he was to return to the battlefield. Ethel once again had money—a ring paper that she could draw her husband's wage on.

She politely refused Ray's offer to live with his parents, telling him she would wait for his return to meet them. Instead, she found a cheap room in the lodging house of a Mrs Skerratt, within walking distance of the Blackpool Promenade.

Mrs Skerratt was nice enough, always complimenting Ethel on how she looked, and wasn't intrusive, so Ethel came to look upon Mrs Skerratt more as a friend than a landlady.

Ethel had wonderful memories of her childhood holidays in Blackpool. Once a year the big cotton mills in Manchester would shut down for maintenance, for what was called 'wakes week', and all the staff would flock to Blackpool or Southport for a holiday. Each town or mill would take a separate week off between July and September, and the seaside towns thrived. These were happy times for Ethel—even after her little sister arrived—as there was always so much to see and do.

Now, having her own room and having to feed herself, Ethel didn't have as much money as she would have liked, but she still dolled herself up and socialised. She was restless, and didn't like things standing still.

She decided it was time to write to her father, to let her family know she was safe, and to ask what had become of her son. She had yet to mention baby Frank to her new husband, but Ray seemed so kind, she was sure he would welcome Frank into their family. No point telling him until he returned; she'd deal with it then.

She filled her days going to the shops, the movies and the theatre. On tour in the town at that time was a popular actress who shared her new name, Ethel Ward. Curious, Ethel took in her show at the Majestic Theatre, and watched the elegantly dressed Miss Ward on stage playing the lead role in a romantic drama. Miss Ward's hair was piled high, with lace covering her shoulders and long neck as she played the wronged woman with style and grace. Ethel felt that was *her* up on that stage; it was *her* drama she was watching unfold, an innocent woman scorned by a cruel man, in her case Billy.

From then on she avidly followed Miss Ward's reviews and write-ups in the newspapers. She wasn't interested in politics and politicians, intellectuals, what was happening on the Front—she preferred the papers that covered fashion and the goings-on and gossip about famous people, rich people and movie stars. She loved reading the descriptive articles, using her imagination to read between the lines. The actress Miss Ward was based in the Midlands, and Ethel would eagerly read what dramas she was headlining in, both on and off the stage.

Then Ethel started going out at night, pretending to be the young actress, dyeing her hair chestnut and wearing it in the same style as Miss Ward. She could often be found in the company of soldiers and sailors on leave, despite her husband still being at the Front. She had always preferred the company of men, especially those who paid her a lot of attention and spent money on her.

Ethel told the men various stories about herself—she was sometimes an actress, sometimes an artist, but most often her story was that her husband had been killed at the Front and that she was there to forget; at that time Blackpool was full of people trying to forget there was a war going on.

After hearing of her husband's death, one soldier, ironically called Smith, felt sorry enough for Ethel that before returning to battle he organised a ring paper for her, stating on it that she was his wife. Ethel conveniently forgot to mention her husband,

Ray Ward, to Private Jack Smith, and now she had two lots of wages to draw on, though she would have to be careful to go to the correct post office with each.

Letters would arrive from Ray and she'd send back brief replies, filled with love and stories about how wonderful life was in Blackpool, omitting the fact that she was entertaining other men. She saw it as her duty to make them feel better and forget about the war—and besides, they looked after her.

Blackpool was busy, there was always something going on. On one occasion she even watched a pilot on leave land his plane on the main beach, before walking into one of the pubs for a drink. The hotels were still running, the restaurants were full, even with war rationing; the ballrooms played music and were filled with dancers. Even the shops had stuff on offer. Exciting things were always happening. Blackpool was the perfect place to forget.

Ethel always felt better going shopping, and it helped fuel her fantasy life—and with two ring papers to draw on, she could spend a bit more on things she wanted. Rather than move to finer lodgings, her extra money was spent on more clothes, and visits to the beautician and hairdresser. After all, she needed to look like the star she was.

But it was never enough, and soon she started telling her fantastic stories to the shop owners. One of her favourite shops was behind the Promenade, near the Winter Gardens. The owner, Mrs Hall, happily listened to her regular customer Mrs Ward, a war widow who had tragically lost her first husband, but had again found happiness with her second, a wealthy decorated army officer. Mrs Ward spent up big, and Mrs Hall did not hesitate to offer her a line of credit. Ethel loved that shop and purchased numerous outfits, hats, bags, shoes and even a bright red feather boa, just like the Hollywood actresses wore. But after racking up an account close to £20 (over $2000 in today's money), Ethel stopped going to the shop, and Mrs Hall began to wonder if the fabulous Mrs Ward was ever going to settle her account.

One Saturday evening, at one of the classier dance halls, Mr and Mrs Hall were seated at a table close to the dance floor when a flash of red whirled past. There in the arms of a uniformed sailor was a laughing Mrs Ward, wearing the red feather boa she still hadn't paid for. As the dancing couple made their way past the Halls' table, Ethel gave the shop owner a quick smile. The shopkeeper glared in return and watched as the couple finished their dance and made their way to their own table, the sailor's arm slipping comfortably over Ethel's shoulders.

———

The following Monday morning, Ethel woke late. The weekend had been a whirlwind of fun—she had met a charming sailor and they had laughed and danced the entire weekend. He had left with promises of seeing her again when he was next on leave. She stretched out under the bedcovers, wondering what she would do that day, when she heard the post arrive.

Dressing with her usual care and attention, she made her way downstairs to see what was in the mail. It was usually only bills, which she would ignore for as long as possible, but today a letter sat on the doormat, bearing her father's familiar hand-writing. She scooped it up to open it, but a feeling of dread stopped her; this was real life.

She made her way to the kitchen and put the letter on the table, busying herself making a pot of tea. While waiting for the water to boil she stared at the letter. Her father would be upset with her, but he would forgive her; he always had. She could explain.

Ethel suddenly snatched the letter up, turned it over, took a deep breath, and then slowly, carefully, opened it. She pulled the single page out and started reading her father's neat writing, covering just about every space of the frail piece of paper, but the words and letters seemed to be jumbled up, dancing before her eyes; she couldn't believe what she was reading. She sat down at the table and forced herself to start again at the beginning. Her father was concerned about her; baby Frank was now living with her in-laws. But the one sentence that caused her the most consternation was, 'Alec is alive.' He had been wounded, but was in hospital, wanting to know where she was. Her father insisted she come home immediately.

Alec was alive? So many emotions raced through her—happiness, shame, anger, fear. How could he be alive? How could she face him? No—he wasn't alive; it was her father trying to get her home. Alec was dead.

She sat down heavily at the table, and through her jumbled thoughts heard the doorbell ring. Almost in a trance she stood to go and answer it, slipping the letter back into its envelope. The doorbell rang again impatiently. Still feeling a little dazed and confused, she opened the door and to her surprise found two policemen standing on the doorstep.

'Mrs Ward?' the taller one asked. 'Mrs Ethel Ward?'

Ethel stood dumbfounded. Was that her?

'Are you Ethel Ward?' he again asked. She could only nod.

'You're under arrest for obtaining goods under false pretences,' he announced. She stood stock-still and stared at the pair of them.

'I, uh I,' she shook her head. 'I'm sorry gentlemen, there must be a mistake,' she replied.

'You are Mrs Ethel Ward, wife of Raymond Ward?' the constable asked again.

She nodded her head slowly, yes, she was.

'You are under arrest for obtaining goods under false pretences from a Mrs Hall on Birley Street,' the man said. 'Mrs Ward, you need to accompany us to the station.'

Ethel couldn't think of anything to say, so she again simply nodded.

'I need to get my coat,' she finally managed in a quiet voice. The police followed her into the house as she went into the kitchen and took the kettle off the stove, grabbing her father's letter and turning to go up the stairs. 'I won't be a moment,' she said, turning to them, smiling sweetly.

To her annoyance they followed her up to her room and watched as she fished her coat out from under a pile of clothes and picked up her handbag. She looked in the mirror and automatically searched out a lipstick from her bag and shakily applied it to her pale lips.

The shorter constable spoke for the first time. 'Come on, Mrs Ward, we don't have all day!'

Ethel looked around her messy room, then walked between the policemen as they headed back downstairs and out the front door.

The court case was all a bit of a blur to Ethel. She kept thinking about her father's letter, which she had read and re-read while stuck in the watchhouse. The dark, cramped cell matched her mood, the grim warden she all but ignored as she gazed at her father's handwriting trying to figure out what to do. It couldn't be right—surely her father was mistaken. But what if he was telling the truth, and it wasn't a ruse just to get her back home? How could she face Alec and her son?

Mrs Hall stood in court and told the story Ethel had given her, finishing her evidence by recounting the shameless behaviour she had witnessed at the Blackpool ballroom. Ethel's landlady, Mrs Skerratt, then stood up and happily told all about Ethel's vast array of beautiful new clothing and costume jewellery, and most damningly, men staying at her establishment in the company of Mrs Ward. Some friend she turned out to be.

Ethel sat in the dock, half listening to the magistrate, lawyer and everyone drone on about her behaviour, just wishing they would be quiet. Her arrest had made the evening papers, and everyone in the crowded courtroom seemed to be staring at her, her world closing in; she felt so let down, by Mrs Hall, Mrs Skerratt and even her own father.

Eventually Ethel was asked to stand. She pushed herself up and forced herself to listen to the magistrate. 'Mrs Ward, you have had very little to say for yourself in this case, but your father-in-law has spoken with me,' he stated.

Ethel stared at him, trying to hide her surprise. Her father-in-law? But Alec's father was still at the Western Front, surely.

'Mr Ward has assured me he will take responsibility for you and make recompense,' he continued.

Mr Ward? *Ray's* father? She quickly looked around the courtroom before the magistrate continued: 'I will therefore place you on a two-year bond to be of good behaviour and that £10 compensation be paid to the prosecutrix Mrs Hall.' He stopped and looked at her expectantly.

'Thank you, Your Honour,' she blurted. She looked around the court again in confusion and waited for the magistrate to leave before she was shown out.

There, standing in the hall, was an older and slightly stooped version of her husband Ray, staring as she approached.

'Mr Ward?' she asked uncertainly.

'Yes,' he replied.

She stood awkwardly in front of him and was unusually lost for words. He grabbed her by the elbow. 'I need to take you home,' he ordered, leading her out of the building. Her mind raced. She was free—but free to do what, go where?

She stopped. 'Mr Ward, I need to thank you for coming and helping me, but I will be fine now.'

Her father-in-law seemed to look right through her. '*You!* You have brought disrepute onto our family, young lady!' he thundered.

Ethel didn't know how to reply. All the time she had spent in the cells, she had been focusing on trying to explain everything to Alec and the *Carter* family, not Ray's.

Mr Ward again pulled her roughly by the elbow.

'I have the most wonderful present for Ray when he returns,' she said suddenly. 'It is in my rooms.'

Mr Ward stopped and stared at her in disbelief as they stood on the busy pavement.

'Could we go and collect it?' she asked meekly, to his grim-set face. He looked about to refuse, so she tried again. 'And, I, I need to collect my things.'

Mr Ward sighed heavily. 'Where are you staying?'

'Not far from here,' she replied sweetly, feeling a little more in control. 'I'll show you,' she said, walking off in front of him.

They arrived at her lodgings and Ethel let them in, glad to see Mrs Skerratt hadn't yet returned. She made her way up the stairs, with Mr Ward senior following.

Entering her room, Ethel was conscious of the unmade bed and clothes strewn around the floor, as her father-in-law looked around in disgust. She grabbed a carpetbag, opened the wardrobe, and they both looked at her vast array of clothes.

'You won't fit them all in that,' Mr Ward said in annoyance, indicating her bag. 'Don't you have anything bigger?' She shook her head and looked sadly at him.

He looked at the bag, then the wardrobe and back again in exasperation. 'You sort through them and I'll find another bag. We won't be able to take it all—you decide what you want to leave. I will be back shortly.'

Ethel heard him go down the stairs and the front door close. She grabbed the most expensive items and shoved them in her carpetbag, looking wistfully at all the marvellous clothes, hats, coats and shoes she would have to leave behind.

Hurriedly, she closed her bag, shut the door behind her, and was gone.

6

MRS LEE

Ethel was on the street, struggling with her overstuffed bag, making her way to the train to make her escape, unsure where exactly that would be.

'You right there, Miss?' a man asked.

He was a good foot shorter than she was, and had an older face. Ethel thought he looked familiar, but was eager to board the train before Mr Ward realised she'd gone. 'Fine, thank you,' she replied in her poshest voice, as she tried to move on.

He stepped in her way. Ethel stopped and looked around nervously, then stood tall and stared down at him. 'Excuse me,' she began, 'I need to make the train.'

Slowly, deliberately, he looked at her and smiled. 'You're in a hurry,' he observed. 'Been watching you for a while,' he added. 'You're pretty good at getting things out of them servicemen.'

'How dare you!' she whispered.

'I can help you,' he whispered back with a wicked grin. 'Saw the coppers pick you up—you need somewhere to hide?'

There must have been something about Fred Lee, because Ethel stayed with him for a few months and worked at an illegal gambling establishment he was running, a place called The Casino on Pleasure Beach. It was straight out of a movie, though perhaps not as glamorous as she would have liked. She initially saw herself as the poor little rich girl who had fallen on hard times, and was under the influence of bad men, but she would redeem herself, once she had the money and means.

Ethel's main job was to assess the punters, size them up, check out how much cash they had on them, and if she thought them a light touch, invite them in for a game of cards. What started off as a convenient place to stay and earn money, quickly turned into an opportunity for her to learn how to cheat at cards and fleece servicemen out of their pay. She was playing the role of a femme fatale, and revelling in it.

As well as money she earned with Fred Lee, she was still drawing on two ring papers, as Mrs Ward and Mrs Smith. She enjoyed dressing up, disguising herself, wearing wigs and heavy make-up. She did, however, avoid distinctive clothing that stood out, worried that maybe Mrs Hall or someone else would recognise her.

She was managing just fine, until she turned up at the post office where she was known as Mrs Ward, and presented the puzzled postmistress with the ring papers for a Mrs Smith. Realising her mistake, she grabbed the ring paper back and left the post office as quickly as she could.

An angry Fred promptly sent her off to stay with friends of his in London, then on to Felixstowe in Suffolk, on the other side of the country, telling her to get rid of Jack Smith's ring paper, as she didn't have a marriage certificate to back it up—advice she didn't immediately follow.

Felixstowe was not nearly as glamorous as Blackpool, nor as much fun, but at least she was safe. A new place, a new name. She was now Mrs Ethel Stevens, staying with Fred's mate Ernie Stevens, but for the new nominated post office at Bent Hill right near the beach, she was Mrs Ward.

Ethel had money and somewhere to stay, but it wasn't long before she once again became bored and restless. After a few weeks she started to travel around the surrounding towns, shopping of course, but the shops were pretty bare, with the war still on—not nearly as much on offer as in Blackpool. One day she took a bus a little further afield, to Southend-on-Sea, and found a dress shop, where she saw the *sweetest* hat. She had to have it, but knew she couldn't afford both the hat and the bus fare back, so decided to try her luck. Initially introducing herself as Mrs Stevens, she then fell into her grieving war-widow story, but midway through slipped up by calling her brave husband Corporal Ward. Instantly suspicious, the shopkeeper, a Mrs Wilburn, queried the different surnames. So Ethel ended up walking out of the store without the hat, with the shopkeeper's accusations ringing in her ears.

Annoyed with herself, Ethel made her way to the bus stop to wait for the bus. How could she have made such a stupid mistake? She should have thought her story through a bit better—she would next time, she vowed. It was February and cold, and Ethel pulled her thick coat tight against the wind. She'd really wanted that hat! It was similar to one she had seen her favourite movie star at the time, Mary Pickford, wear; it would have looked wonderful with her outfit, and was warmer than the one she was currently wearing. She shuffled her feet and huddled down under the bus shelter to wait.

'Mrs Stevens?' a male voice asked. Ethel stiffened and didn't know whether to look up or ignore what was obviously not her name.

'Mrs Ward?' the voice asked again. She looked up to see a tall, middle-aged bobby standing before her.

'No, sorry,' she said, turning away.

The policeman looked across the road. Ethel followed his gaze and saw the cranky shopkeeper watching them both.

'Is this her?' he shouted. The well-dressed Mrs Wilburn nodded her head.

'You'd better come with me, Miss,' he said, reaching down and grabbing Ethel's arm.

———•··•———

At the police station, they went through her bag and found two ring papers—one in the name of Ward, the other Smith. And Ethel had been using the surname Stevens, so she was in trouble again.

She tried to explain her way out of the situation, but rather than listen to her, they locked her up and contacted the police in Blackpool, as, according to the dates, that was where she had last used the two ring papers together. Blackpool sent back a telegram: a detective was on his way.

Ethel had plenty of time to ponder her predicament. She'd found the second ring paper and was going to hand it in—that was what she'd tell them—but when she tried it out on the local bobbies, they wouldn't listen to her: 'Tell it to the judge!' they said. She managed to get a message to Ernie Stevens, asking him to come and bail her out, but when the police knocked on his door with a few questions, he said he'd never even met her. So she had to sit in frustration and wait for the detective to arrive.

Three days she waited in her cell.

When Detective Carter finally arrived and introduced himself, she stopped herself from remarking on his surname, though it did amuse her. These policemen were completely unaware of her first marriage—best to keep it that way!

Detective Carter was a thin, serious-looking man, with gaunt, hollowed-out cheeks and thin black hair plastered to his scalp. Noting the wedding ring on his left hand, Ethel couldn't help feeling a bit sorry for his wife.

After completing lengthy paperwork, she and the detective boarded the train to London, heading back to Blackpool, where she knew she would have to face court again, and what would surely be a big fine. Fred Lee would help her get out on bail, she hoped, but she knew he'd be angry with her—he had, after all, told her to destroy Jack Smith's ring paper.

On the train Ethel tried to make conversation with Detective Carter. After the first hour, he finally began answering her queries, albeit reluctantly. She asked about his family, where he lived, did he enjoy his job. Each of his answers was civil but brief, but Ethel thought he was warming to her. She gently placed her hand on his upper thigh and asked, 'Can I make it worth your while if you destroy those ring papers?' as if asking to borrow his newspaper.

He looked at her in surprise—and then, to her amusement, horror. 'That is impossible,' was all he said, so Ethel tried again.

'Surely you could destroy one of those papers, the one for Jack Smith, and make it all right with the inspector at Southend, and I can see you after . . .' she cooed sweetly, giving him one of her disarming looks with her big blue eyes.

He refused to talk to her after that.

Back in Blackpool, she tried in vain to get in touch with Fred Lee, but he didn't post bail, so she had to wait in the cells.

At her court case a week later, Ethel stood before the magistrate and implored him to believe that she had only drawn money on one ring paper, under her married name of Ethel Ward—which was the truth when she was back in Felixstowe, but not in Blackpool; she generally had some truth in her stories, most of the time. She then said she'd found the ring paper of Jack Smith and had kept it, wanting to find the real Mrs Smith and hand it to her in person.

After she finished, the Public Prosecutor Mr Callis brought in a witness from the registry office where she and Ray Ward were married, to confirm who she was. He then brought in Mrs Gertrude Dennison from the Revoe Post Office in Blackpool, where she'd been Mrs Smith—and Mrs Alice Fitchell from the

Fleetwood Post Office seven miles north of Blackpool, where she was Mrs Ward. They both testified that the lady before them was indeed the one who had drawn money using both ring papers. Mrs Fitchell then told them that the woman in court, who she knew as Mrs Ward, had presented Smith's ring paper instead of Ward's on her last visit; Mrs Fitchell had then promptly reported the attempted fraud to the authorities and the War Office.

Detective Carter then took the stand and told them all about Ethel's proposal in the train back to Blackpool, to lose Jack Smith's ring paper in return for a sexual liaison.

After Detective Carter had stepped down, the disgusted magistrate addressed Ethel directly, saying she was a very dangerous woman, and asking if she had anything to say to the court.

'I want to tell you the truth!' Ethel blurted out. 'I was never married to Corporal Smith,' she said elevating Jack Smith's rank from Private. 'I was ashamed to tell you before, or to even tell my relatives. I lived with him for a short time,' she admitted meekly, 'but my marriage to Corporal Ward was a legal one.'

'*Was* legal, Mrs Ward? Surely you are still married to him?' the prosecutor asked sharply, leaving Ethel flustering for an answer.

'Yes, of course,' she replied. So much for trying to tell the truth. She probably would have been better off not saying anything at all.

When the magistrate asked her to rise for his decision, Ethel was thinking she could borrow money from Fred to pay the fine, even though he hadn't put up her bail or even come to see her since her return. She even half expected Mr Ward to be there in court to bail her out again, but this time she was on her own.

She stood while the magistrate droned on about her despicable fraudulent behaviour, waiting for it all to be over. Fraud cases involving ring papers were starting to become a problem. A ring paper could be stolen and the thief then nominating a different post office could draw funds for some time before the duplicity was found. It was a problem the magistrate and government wanted to deter.

For obtaining sums of money amounting to nearly £30 from the War Office using Jack Smith's ring paper, the magistrate ordered she serve six months hard labour at the infamous Strangeways Prison.

On hearing this appalling news, Ethel promptly fainted.

7

MRS SPURGESS

Three hundred women were housed in four wings at Strangeways, the notorious home of murderers and Irish political prisoners. Ethel was in there for swindling a few extra dollars, not killing anyone—to her, it all seemed very unjust.

Strangeways in Manchester was cramped, dark and damp, and her stint there was the lowest point of Ethel's life. The other female prisoners were horrible, the wardens cruel, and the work monotonous and hard. The single cells were long and thin, measuring twelve feet by seven feet, and nine feet high. A folding bench was both her mattress base at night and table during the day, when she had to strap the mattress to the wall each morning. She had one blanket at night, no pillow, a small cupboard, a three-legged stool and a smelly privy in the corner. For the next six months she ate to feel better, taking extra servings of the often fatty meals; there was nothing else that made her feel good in the whole place. She learnt to clean floors really well, and was glad when her time was finally up.

Ethel's family certainly didn't know she'd been in prison, so when she was released in the late summer of 1918, she set off for London, where she met up with Fred Lee, who had moved down from Blackpool. He explained why he hadn't come to bail her out in Blackpool—he'd been in London by that stage and couldn't return.

Accepting his half-hearted apology, Ethel began working with Fred on a new scheme, going out with well-heeled servicemen who were on rest and recreation leave to relieve them of their funds. Fred would introduce her to poor blokes straight off the Western Front, she'd charm them and tell them she wanted to marry them, then ask for money for wedding clothes and an engagement ring, before finally disappearing, leaving the men wondering what had happened. Fred would look out for her and they'd split the money.

When the Great War ended on 11 November 1918, she'd just about had enough of Fred Lee—so the next day she plucked up her nerve and went home to Manchester for a visit. It was time to get her life back.

Her mother and young sister hardly spoke to her when Ethel first arrived unannounced, but her father was delighted to see her safe and well. The more offhanded her mother acted towards her, the more she wanted to impress.

Ethel told them she'd been working with the Foreign Office as an undercover spy, journeying into France and Belgium incognito as a commercial traveller. Her story was padded out with details about different places she had heard about from the returned servicemen she'd fleeced in London—street names, famous places, vivid descriptions of war-torn lands used to impress a girl back home. She liked the sound of her own story, the brave secret spy, though she presented herself as a more demure Mata Hari for her family's sake.

Her mother had scoffed in disbelief; her father beamed with pride. They had last heard from her as the newly married Mrs Ward living it up in Blackpool well over a year before, and nothing since. Her mother scolded Ethel for having left her baby; her father Frank defended her. When her mother started on about her bigamous marriage to Ray Ward, Ethel finally turned to face her.

'I thought Alec was *dead*!' she yelled. 'I didn't know, I couldn't . . .' she burst into tears, letting them flow freely, before burrowing her head into her father's shoulder.

'And what of your child, and your rightful husband?' her mother demanded. Ethel howled loudly into her father's shoulder.

'That is enough Elizabeth, can you not see that Ethel is upset?' her father said.

Her mother went rigid. 'I certainly can Frank, but why didn't our daughter get in touch with Alec and come back to her child when she knew the truth?'

Ethel looked up at her mother and realised there was no hope from that quarter, turning instead to her father.

'I didn't know, Daddy, please believe me, I thought Alec was dead, and then, I . . . I was so ashamed . . . I threw myself into . . . into my work . . . my war work, instead,' she said between sniffles.

'Of course you did, my dear girl,' her father said, patting her gently on the back. 'Of course you did.'

Hands on her hips, Elizabeth glared at her daughter. 'So, what are you going to do now?' she demanded. 'Alec wants a *divorce*, you need to fix up this mess!'

Ethel pulled away from her father and looked at Elizabeth meekly. 'I will, Mother, I didn't know, I truly didn't know—I'll go and see Alec now.'

Elizabeth visibly relaxed, and Ethel suppressed a smile, surprised how easily she had managed to calm her mother simply by telling her what she wanted to hear.

Ethel picked up her bag and went straight to the front door. As she turned the handle, she felt her father's hand on her arm.

'Do you have money?' he asked, and she shook her head, looking down at the floor, though she probably did have a stash in her bag. Her father opened his wallet and took out a new £5 note, and pushed it into her hand.

'Come back and tell us how you go,' he said, opening the door for her. 'Do you want me to come with you?'

She shook her head.

'No, I need to do this alone.'

He nodded sadly.

Ethel caught the next train back to London, and spent her father's money on fancy shoes, a smart new coat and matching hat, with change to spare. The war was over and returned servicemen were everywhere.

On 14 November she married Private Al Spurgess. They drank and partied with the rest of the country in celebration, and when her new husband's finances ran out, so did she.

8

MRS GIBLETT

Ethel was on her first outing in another new outfit to celebrate the last of her father's money when she met Captain William Thornton 'Norman' Giblett, who was waiting to be sent back home to Australia. Tall, dark and handsome, Norman Giblett was her ticket away from the mess in England.

Norm had been one of the first to sign up when war was declared. He was in the first landing at Gallipoli and was quickly promoted to Second Lieutenant, before evacuating with the rest of the troops and being sent to the Western Front. There he was promoted to Lieutenant and then Captain, and was awarded the Military Cross and Bar for Gallantry in September 1917 at the Battle of Polygon Wood. He had everything Ethel was after: security, respectability, good looks; he was even a proper war hero. All of that, *and* the prospect of starting a new life in a new country.

Her name was Daphne Pollard, she told him with a laugh when they first met—yes, just like the Australian silent movie star, though Pollard was her married name. Her husband had perished early on in the war and both of her parents were dead, though her father Frank had been a successful cotton buyer. She repeated her story of working for the Foreign Office, exaggerating it even further: she had travelled incognito regularly to the Continent as a commercial traveller, taking back vital information to England. And now the war was over, she was uncertain what she would do.

Captain Giblett fell for the eloquent, brave war widow and her story, and when she suggested marriage, he happily agreed—it was time to celebrate life after the war. He asked if she wanted to marry in a church, but she shook her head, telling him that she had been married in a big church before and she didn't really need to do all that again. And besides, she didn't have any family left and his were so far away; a nice quiet ceremony was all she wanted—though she did need an engagement ring and a new dress, and perhaps shoes and a bag to match.

They married in the registry office at Warminster and rented a large home at The Bungalow in Ballington as they waited for a berth on one of the ships returning servicemen to Australia. While they waited, Captain Giblett eagerly told his new bride more about his home and family.

'We'll live in Thornleigh in Sydney, where I grew up,' he explained. 'I'll probably go back to working in my father's shop, which is also the post office.'

'Tell me about your parents. Do you think they'll like me?'
Ethel asked.

'Of course they will,' Norm replied, placing his arm around
her shoulders reassuringly in the drawing room of their first
home. 'What is there not to like?'

In June 1919 they finally left England on board the troopship *Katoomba* to Sydney, where his parents greeted them at
the docks, eager to meet this lovely English girl their son had
married and to welcome them both home.

Ethel happily started to settle into life on the outskirts of
Sydney as Mrs Daphne Giblett, and was getting used to her
new name and their respectable social standing in the close-
knit community. Her husband built them a new weatherboard
house in Short Street, Thornleigh, walking distance from his
father's store. Their brand new home had all the mod cons, a
gas stove and lights, and was decked out just how she wanted it.

Ethel really wanted this marriage, this new identity, this new
shot at life to work—but she wasn't prepared for how dull life
in the outer suburbs would be, especially as Norm kept a tight
string on their finances.

She was pleased though when Norm took over the Thornleigh Post Office and General Store from his father the following
year; she was now a respectable postmistress, working alongside her husband, and was getting quite good at sidling a little
cash away for herself so that she had some spending money. But
all that ended when Norm hired another former army mate to
help him out, relegating Ethel back to the role of doting wife.

She began taking the train into the city as regularly as
possible, and eventually convinced Norm that being in an

empty house in the outer suburbs wasn't for her. He rented her a small house in busy Falcon Street, North Sydney, across the harbour from the city, and he would catch the train down from Thornleigh and visit her on weekends.

From her new home she wrote to her father, explaining that things hadn't worked out between her and Alec, and that she had married a decorated captain from Australia and was now living in marital bliss in Sydney, apologising that it had all been a bit of a rush, but that she was happy.

Her father replied promptly. He was glad she was safe and well, but worried about her and his grandson, Frank Carter. Ethel hadn't even thought about her son since she had left, and wrote back to her father that baby Frank was better off without her, and that she had a new chance at happiness. Her father replied, saying he just wanted her to be happy, and they kept corresponding from then on, Ethel relating wonderful stories of her new life in far away Australia, and her father telling her about life back in England.

Unfortunately for Ethel, on one visit to Falcon Street, Norm happened to come across her father's letters, placed carefully back in their envelopes and tied together with a ribbon. She instantly snatched them away from him, ran into the lounge room and threw them in the fire burning in the grate—but not before he saw the sender's name and address: Mr Frank Swindells, Manchester.

Incensed, Norm demanded she tell him what she was hiding.

Giving her best theatrical performance, Ethel stood in front of him and burst into tears. 'It's just memories from home . . . from my time before the war,' she managed to get out. 'It is nothing important, just news—I . . . I'm glad I'm here with you, Norman,' she sobbed, looking up at him through tear-filled eyes.

He looked at her for a moment, then opened his arms for her. Ethel rushed into them, forgiven.

But Norm was suspicious after that, and on another visit to Falcon Street found blotting paper she had been using to dry the ink on her letters to her father. Using a mirror he read enough of the reversed scraps of her handwriting to work out her father was alive.

How could she be writing letters to her father, when he was supposed to be dead? Norm interrogated her, shooting question after question at her until he had all the details he wanted.

She decided to come clean. Her parents were alive. Her name was not Daphne Pollard, as she had claimed when they first met, but Florence Elizabeth Ethel Swindells, then Carter by marriage. She had married Alexander Carter when she was young, at the start of the war, and they had one child, Frank. She tried in vain to tell Norm she thought her first husband dead when she went off working for the War Office, but he wouldn't have it: the War Office would have informed her when he was found alive, he shot back at her, so of course she would have known.

When asked about her child Frank, she told Norman she thought he was probably living with his father, who had filed for divorce on desertion allegations, but admitted she hadn't signed the papers when she became Mrs Giblett.

That was the last straw: she was a bigamist and she had known.

Norm was furious, and despite Ethel's best pleas, left.

———•·•———

Within a week, Ethel was presented with Norman's divorce papers.

After seeking her own legal advice, Ethel sent Norman a typed letter, imploring him to return, and assuring him she would do *'all in my power to make you happy'*.

She didn't have to wait long for his handwritten reply.

Thornleigh
Feb. 3rd 1922

Dear Daphne,

In answer to your letter, I refuse to return.

Yours sincerely,
N. Giblett

After three years, her marriage to Norman Giblett, and hope of a new life, was over.

9

MRS HOURN

Ethel booked herself into the fashionable Australia Hotel, across the harbour into the heart of the city, again using the movie-star name Daphne Pollard. With its modern plumbing, stylish decor and imposing staircase inside the grand entrance, the Australia was *the* place to stay in Sydney. It looked like it was straight out of a movie set, and all the best travellers stayed there.

Within weeks Ethel had bewitched another decorated soldier, Captain Midford Stanley 'Stan' Hourn. His family and friends were delighted with the charming young English lady Stan was marrying, and in celebration held a fashionable handkerchief party that made the social pages in the women's section of the local newspapers, to Ethel's delight.

Ethel finally got her big church wedding, on 2 May 1923, at the Methodist Church in the city. Mr and Mrs Hourn moved out to the suburbs, and within days of their marriage Ethel had stripped her unfortunate new husband of cash and vanished again.

After his wife disappeared with his life savings, Stan searched the suburbs around Belmore, where he lived, and travelled into the city, but she was nowhere to be found. He asked all who may have known her where Daphne may have gone, including the young lady who had witnessed their marriage, Mona Lambert—but even she had to admit only knowing the charming Daphne a short time.

Not long after, Stan received a telegram from Ethel in Brisbane informing him the marriage was over, and asking him to send her belongings and wedding dress back to her. She insisted there was no hope of reconciliation.

In late May, he was reading the *Sydney Morning Herald* over breakfast when an article on the front page caught his eye. It was about a peculiar upcoming case of bigamy, being brought by William Thornton Giblett against an English girl whose divorce was not absolute when they married in 1919. The girl was Florence Elizabeth Ethel Carter, formerly Swindells, falsely calling herself Daphne Vivienne Pollard—the same name as his wife! It couldn't be.

Stan noted the date and fronted to the Divorce Court, where he learnt that he too had been a victim of bigamy, confirmed with a photograph of his smiling wife supplied by her other hapless husband.

Captain Giblett secured the order for nullity of marriage, but it would take poor Stan many years until he was able to do the same.

———·—

Ethel, meanwhile, was on her way back to England; she'd had enough of Australia. And she was travelling first class—much better than her trip out on the troopship with Norm—on the SS *Suevic,* a jubilee-class White Star ship, built by the same company as the ill-fated *Titanic,* sailing from Brisbane via Perth, South Africa and on to Southampton.

On board she socialised with the other first-class passengers and told them a fanciful tale about being a war widow whose brave husband had been killed; now wanting to forget, she was on a world trip and was heading back home. Her parents were both dead, she told them: her father, a doctor in the Great War, had perished in France, while her mother, a cousin of the famous Coats cotton family, had died when she was quite young (Coats was a more recognisable name than Swindells outside of England).

With her smooth-talking charm, elegant clothing and regal manner, they readily believed her tragic tale and welcomed her into their social circle. This was where she believed she belonged in society—not gaol, or living in some dreary suburb. She was living the high life, just like a movie star. All it took was money to buy the passage, and she had the lifestyle that she craved and felt she deserved.

On the deck most days, the young men would play cricket, which the ladies would watch as they had their high tea; in the evenings there were fancy dress balls, music and dancing, and they played cards and parlour games. Ethel found the entire trip both fun and luxurious as she dined and partied all the way back to England.

In London she booked herself into The Strand and went looking for her next husband among its well-heeled clientele.

Little did she know at the time, but she'd brought back a little souvenir to always remember that luxurious trip back from Australia.

10

MRS ANDERSON

At The Strand, Ethel met an Australian businessman, George 'Addie' Anderson. He was fifteen years older than her, and a man of the world.

They married in March 1924 , and on 12 October that year, her little surprise souvenir from her voyage back to England was born, Frank George Anderson. Ethel had given her second son the same first name as her first child, in honour of her beloved father. Ethel's marriage certificate was issued in South Dublin, Ireland, as was Frank's birth certificate, which listed George Anderson, occupation salesman, as his father; even though Ethel and George met and married just over six months before he was born.

Mr Anderson travelled the world, or so she liked to tell everyone, taking his new bride on overseas trips, always first class on the best liners. She loved first class. They travelled with lords, ladies, the rich and famous, to New York regularly, only staying about a week before sailing back.

In 1925, when baby Frank was just five months old, they sailed to exotic, far-away Shanghai. Ethel was thrilled to find Lord Cavan, chief of the Imperial Staff and good friend to the King, on board with his young wife and their baby, Elizabeth, who was only a month older than Frank. She was sad to see Lady Cavan and her family leave at Gibraltar without exchanging particulars, but perhaps Lord Cavan could pick an upstart, and stopped any association before it even began. Still, the name Lady Cavan was to feature in her most impressive tales from then on, in her eyes, they were firm friends.

Their own journey then continued on through the Suez Canal to Singapore, Hong Kong and then finally Shanghai.

This was the height of the roaring twenties, with Shanghai full of Americans, the French, English, and even White Russians who had fled the 1917 Russian Revolution—with women wearing elegant, fashionable dresses, and spiffs parading around the streets in their flashy get-ups as they enjoyed everything Shanghai had on offer. There were cocktail parties at sunset, jazz playing in smoke-filled nightclubs, entertainment of every kind on offer. The twenties in Shanghai was a cosmopolitan, freewheeling powerhouse of entertainment, opium and gambling.

What George Anderson sold for a living was never entirely clear, but even with a small baby in tow, Ethel was having the time of her life.

They were only in Shanghai a month when Ethel found out she was pregnant again. The decision was made for her to return to England with Frank to have the baby, leaving her husband George in Shanghai.

———·•·———

Ethel's third baby boy, William Basil Dwight Anderson, was born at Streatham Manor on 15 December 1925. After World War I, it had developed into the entertainment centre for the West End of South London with a large theatre, three cinemas, the Locarno ballroom and an ice rink, but no manor, unless you include the Manor Arms hotel down the road in Mitcham Lane.

On St Patrick's Day, 1927, Ethel and her two young sons left cold, grey London for Sydney, aboard the SS *Baradine*, a slick P&O passenger liner.

Ethel's father, who had paid for their passage to Australia, sadly waved the little family off as they followed the elusive Mr Anderson back to his home country. The *Baradine* was a migrant ship that gave free passage in third class for nearly 500 migrants travelling to Australia in the lower decks, including a dozen or so young boys known as the Wembley Boys, child migrants from an orphanage.

In the early evenings, Ethel would gently rock little Basil to sleep as Frank lay in his bunk, telling them they'd see their daddy soon. When he was finally asleep, she'd lean over, tuck Frank in tight and give him a peck on the cheek.

'Look after your little brother Frank,' she'd whisper, then head out towards the music.

One night Ethel was standing in the bar immaculately dressed, cigarette in one hand, drink in the other, and surrounded by admiring men, when she eventually noticed Frank, in his pyjamas, standing by the door out to the promenade deck and gave him an annoyed look. She turned to one of the men she'd been talking with, smiled apologetically and handed him her drink and cigarette, and walked towards her son. She scooped him up without a word and walked back out into the sea air towards her crying baby in the distance. She stayed with them after that.

It must have been quite a party ship; two female immigrants had already been put ashore together with a male crew member at Cape Town, when they were found sharing a cabin one evening by the matron accompanying the female single immigrants. Such scandalous, immoral behaviour would not be tolerated.

When they eventually arrived in Sydney, there was nobody to greet their little family.

Ethel was heartbroken and angry. A man had made a fool out of her again, and she had nothing to show for it but two young children.

11

MRS BAKER

Ethel moved in with a Mr Baker, to the beachside suburb of Coogee in Sydney's east. Thick blackberry bushes grew along the nearby cliffs, and while Mr Baker was teaching Ethel to drive, her two young boys would scour the cliff tops by themselves, searching for the sweet berries. Unfortunately for Mr Baker, once Ethel knew how to drive his big pale-blue Studebaker, she packed the boys and their few belongings into it, and simply drove away.

She then rented a flat for them in Rosebank Street, Darling-hurst, just down the road from busy Kings Cross.

Soon afterwards Ethel hired a laundress, a short, dark-haired woman called Maggie, to take their clothes away for washing and pressing. Maggie took more than their clothing, however—she completely cleaned Ethel out.

All her beautiful jewellery that had been given to her by various men over the years—the gold wristlet watch from her father, her gold and platinum twin diamond engagement ring from Stan Hourn, a diamond cluster ring, her emerald engagement ring from Norman Giblett, her engagement ring from George Anderson with five large diamonds set into the wide gold band, the gold and diamond bar brooch Norman gave her when they finished their house in Thornleigh, and a gold fountain pen she'd pocketed on the trip out to Australia the year before.

All gone. All her treasures, all her jewellery, gone. Despite filing a complaint with the local police, all her treasures were lost.

To top it off, she hadn't been able to track down her husband George Anderson. This wouldn't happen until years later, when she found he was married and had other children; ironically, it turned out he was a bigamist as well.

Ethel had had enough. She was leaving Sydney.

Curiously, just before Ethel left again, there was an overnight break-in at Thornleigh, in the shop her previous husband Norm Giblett owned. Police records showed a full week's trading, just over £46, was stolen, but no damage reported.

Just a coincidence, perhaps.

———————

The first night after leaving Sydney, Ethel and the boys slept in Wollongong, in the Studebaker.

The next day they hit the road again and stopped at a picturesque little country town called Cobargo, where there were lots of dairy cows and green grass, with the ocean in the distance.

Next door to the small Catholic Church was an orphanage for approximately 40 boys, run by the nuns at St Joseph's Convent. Large, neatly kept rose bushes, bursting with a rainbow of colours, greeted them as they made their way past the front gate. A tall pine tree could be seen behind the convent, poking over the roof of the single-storey building. It was on the large open verandah, with floors that shone like a palace, that the boys slept on mattresses each night.

This was where Ethel left Frank and Basil, aged just three and four, for the first time.

12

MRS THOMPSON & GLORIA GREY

Ethel sailed back to England. Not having much money, she had to travel third class—they wouldn't even let her on the upper decks!—and vowed to herself that she would never slum it again.

Back in England, she went to her father, explained she was in a pickle, told him about Mr Anderson, and how she had left her two young sons in a boys' home.

He agreed to send £25 (approximately $2400) a month to help support her family, and then told her to go back to Australia and look after her sons.

And return she did—but not before she married William Lloyd Thompson in Manchester, stripped him of cash and spent it on a first class fare back to Australia.

———

One Sunday afternoon, after returning to Australia, Ethel drove the big blue Studebaker to Cobargo, pulling up outside the convent in a cloud of smoke.

There had been a previous Sunday afternoon visit to St Joseph's by Ethel, before she had left for England eight months previous, when she had given her young boys bags of boiled lollies and a tin of marbles for them to play with. She had sat down with them under the pine tree in the garden and showed them how to play marbles, before kissing the top of their heads and driving away in a stream of smoke and dust.

This time she told the nuns she was taking her sons for a short drive in her car around the countryside. Little did they suspect that Ethel had no intention of bringing them back.

That first night they again slept in the car, and the following day were in Melbourne. Ethel found a house in Shelley Street, Elwood, near St Kilda, with the Palais Theatre and Luna Park nearby. Like Blackpool it had a long wooden pier and pavilion, and especially on weekends it was *the* place for Melbournites to relax and have fun.

She added a year on the boy's ages and sent them to Elwood Public School, where they made plenty of friends; their lives were not nearly as strict as the convent had been. Meanwhile, Ethel continued to spend up big.

As usual, she never had enough money for all of the things she wanted, and started wheedling money and goods out of people. She used to catch the tram into the city during the day to shop in swanky establishments, without always paying.

It wasn't long before she was brought before the courts on four charges of false pretences.

She dressed the boys in matching outfits, slicked their hair back and told them to be good, as they were ushered by her solicitor into the Supreme Court building in the heart of Melbourne. 'Whatever you hear, Frank, Basil, don't say a thing. Do you understand?' she warned her boys as they waited outside one of the smaller courtrooms.

The courtroom door opened and a man called out: 'Mrs Gloria Ethel Grey.'

Ethel walked in behind her lawyer, her young boys in tow, then stood with the rest of the court as the judge and a jury of twelve well-dressed men filed in.

Retired Victorian premier and now Chief Justice of Victoria Sir William Irvine sat and listened silently as the four charges of false pretences were read out, giving an insight into why he was nicknamed 'Iceberg' Irvine.

He listened, nodded his head and the case started.

A hairdresser, Madam Du Barry of Swanston Street, stood up, then pointed animatedly and shouted at Ethel as she gave evidence, repeatedly calling her Gloria Grey. Mrs Grey, the hairdresser claimed, had signed useless cheques, and owed her over three pounds. Her's was one of three business houses that had laid claims. 'Maureen', a milliners in Collins Street, was owed 25 shillings for a hat. This was where Ethel had also cashed a valueless cheque for four pounds. And as a lover of all things fashionable and expensive Ethel also owed the 'Gift Salon' in Collins Street over three pounds ($300) for a handbag.

After some time Frank started squirming in his seat and mentioned to his mother quietly that he needed to go to the toilet, so during a break in proceedings, Ethel took her boys to the women's toilets.

'Who's Gloria Grey?' her son Frank asked once they were inside.

Ethel stopped and quickly looked around to make sure no one else was in the toilets. 'Hush now, Frank,' she said sharply, and told him quietly, 'That's just my name sometimes.'

She pulled their jackets straight and looked them over. 'Best behaviour now boys, and don't say another word. Do you understand? It's important.'

———

Gloria Grey was a platinum-blonde American actress with large blue eyes who played romantic action leads in the 1920s. Ethel had seen her play the role of stylish Lady Blanton in the movie *Blake of Scotland Yard*, where the actress chased a bandit through areas of upper-class London, and Ethel's imagination swept her away into the action. She started bleaching her hair and having it cut in a fashionable bob style with a Marcel wave, the same as the young actress—hence all the trips to Madam Du Barry's.

Ethel held a cheque account with the Commercial Bank in Sydney and her cheques didn't have the account owner's name, or any other identification, other than the ornate bank logo and a number on the top left corner. Cheques remained like this for another twenty years. The cheque, when deposited, had to travel to the bank where the account had been opened.

A clerk would then look through ledgers until he found the cheque number and the account it belonged to. The clerk then had to find the ledger that contained the account and draw it against the funds available—and if there wasn't enough money in the account, the cheque would have to travel back to the bank it was deposited in, with an explanatory note stating that there were insufficient funds. The whole process could take up to two weeks depending on how far the cheque had to travel, and the speed of the delivery method used. Back then, people were more inclined to take you on your word—you were who you said you were—but cheques were generally not cashed unless the bank clerk or shop owner knew and trusted the person asking to cash it. It took considerable charm for Ethel to convince so many, so convincingly to take a relative stranger on her word. Perhaps it had started by accident; she may have initially just overspent as her father was still sending money but when the funds were not in the account, the cheques bounced, and when funds were not repaid, the shopkeepers took her to court.

Her lawyer, Mr Bourke, using this argument, told Justice Irvine that Mrs Grey was waiting for remittances from abroad, and she had expected them to be paid into her account. He continued on, explaining that when she drew the cheques she thought the money would be available to meet them.

The lawyer for the creditors, Mr Book, argued that Ethel had signed the cheques three different ways—as Gloria Grey, Ethel Grey and Ethel Anderson—and that trust could not be placed in her.

Ethel was then asked to take the stand; all eyes were on her as she sauntered up into the dock and took an oath. She explained that Anderson was the name of her first husband, and father to her two sons, indicating her boys sitting quietly on either side of the policewoman.

She suddenly burst into tears and stated that Mr Grey was no longer in their lives. It was her father in far away mother England who was now supporting them due to her unfortunate circumstances, and her boys were her only family in Australia. She told them she didn't get the notice from the bank advising her that they had closed the account; otherwise she would have gladly paid.

The jury went out to deliberate. Four hours later they decided she was guilty of fraud on two charges and let her off on the other two, but asked the judge for leniency in sentencing on account of her two young sons.

Through his thin-rimmed glasses, Justice Irvine looked down at the two young boys sitting on either side of their elegantly dressed mother. He cleared his throat.

'You have a bank account, Mrs Grey, and your address is known to your creditors—I do not see you as a dishonest person.'

Ethel smiled uncertainly: having been found guilty on two charges, she had been warned of the prospect of a gaol term by Mr Bourke.

'It was apparent from the evidence that you had reasonable hope of being placed in possession of funds, provided within a day or two or within a very short time,' Justice Irvine continued. He stopped and again cleared his throat.

'Had it not been for the strong recommendation of the jury, I would have felt compelled to impose a period of imprisonment. I instead impose a £50 fine and place you on a good behaviour bond for three years.'

13

MRS GARDINER

Ethel and her boys were on the move again, this time to South Australia, to the small suburb of Henley Beach on the outskirts of Adelaide. Henley Beach sat right up against the sand, and like Blackpool and St Kilda had a big wooden pier, pavilions, a wide esplanade and trams.

Frank and Basil went to school every weekday, and Ethel seemed settled there for a while, making school lunches for the boys, and giving them a sixpence to spend at the shops each day after school.

The Great Depression was starting to really hit, and a large red-headed man named Joseph Gardiner moved in with them. He and Ethel would leave the young boys at home alone for a day or two, sometimes more. Ethel would make sure there was food in the house and a sixpence on the table for every day they'd be away, leaving Frank, aged 6, and Basil, aged 5, to take themselves off to school and feed and care for themselves. By counting up those sixpences the boys knew how long their mother would be gone for.

When Mr Baker's old blue Studebaker finally gasped its last breath, Ethel started using taxis and then a flash car hire company—complete with a uniformed driver—to drive her where she needed to go; after all, having a big car and a driver was what she deserved. After paying her car hire accounts for some time with the money from her father, the company let her have an account—but as cash became tight, the account wasn't always paid.

Ethel was instructed to go to court. She didn't turn up, however, and not long afterwards was picked up by the police.

Joe took the two boys with him to bail her out; paying cash for her bond, and more for the outstanding fine she'd been given at the court case she hadn't attended. Ethel was led out of the holding cells, all the while chatting quite gaily to the police officer who was filling out the ledger, telling him all about herself and her circumstances. She explained that this was her husband Joe, and how he was a war pensioner and held a big station up in Queensland, and all about her two young boys, their names, ages and what they liked to do. She behaved as if she was at a social occasion.

Paperwork completed, she thanked the officer and apologised for any inconvenience she'd caused him, and then merrily waltzed out the door, with Joe and the boys in tow, as if she hadn't been in trouble with the law at all.

———

After one trip away in 1932, as the Great Depression was taking hold around the world, Ethel came home without Joe, agitated and uptight, smoking like a chimney.

One morning, not long afterwards, she made a special effort with her appearance and, unusually, walked the boys to school, taking them by a very indirect route, down the main promenade. They stopped outside the Okeh Café, which had a lovely big delicatessen out the back.

Strolling up to the counter, she enquired in her very proper English if Mr Nobbs was in? No, the lady behind the counter told her, Mr Nobbs was out.

'Oh well, he should know us,' Ethel began. 'My husband Mr Anderson has just left on his way to Gawler. He is a magistrate there, attending a case.' The lady behind the counter appeared impressed. 'Unfortunately,' Ethel continued, 'he has mistakenly taken my wallet with him, and has left me no money to make my purchases for my boys—it is all most inconvenient.' The lady behind the counter looked suitably concerned.

'I'm sorry, I seemed to have missed your name?' Ethel then asked.

'Milly—Milly McCann.'

'Thank you Milly, you have a wonderful array of goods here. I will have to try and get a message to my husband, and call back in,' smiled Ethel. 'Good day to you.'

With that, she led her boys out of the café and finished walking them to school.

Unusually, she was at the school gate that afternoon when the boys were let out of school. They walked back through town, stopping again outside the café, where she told them quietly, 'Not a word boys, on your best behaviour.'

Inside, they waited for Milly to finish serving a customer. Milly saw them and smiled.

'Mrs Anderson,' Milly greeted them.

'Hello again Milly, I have managed to get in touch with my husband and he will come in and cover my purchases on his return,' Ethel said sweetly, 'but he is unable to get back from Gawler until tomorrow night, as the case he is attending has been held over.'

Milly nodded in understanding, falling under Ethel's spell.

'I would like to have some goods until tomorrow; my husband will settle for them then,' Ethel stated with authority, expecting her wish to be granted.

'Certainly Mrs Anderson,' Milly replied, 'I'm sure we can help you out until tomorrow.' She asked Ethel her details, with Ethel supplying a false address.

Milly motioned for them to follow her downstairs, where she introduced Ethel to the manager.

'Lance here will attend to your order, Mrs Anderson,' Milly said. Hearing the bell ring in the shop upstairs, she then turned and headed back up.

Shortly afterwards, Ethel walked out with plenty of groceries, including the biggest and tastiest leg of ham any of them had seen for a long time.

The following day she again escorted her boys to school, stopping outside that same café. She looked at the boys sternly, and they understood not to say a word.

'Ah Milly,' she said as they entered. 'Thank you for your kind assistance yesterday. I'm sure my husband will be in by the end of trade to fix our account, but I wanted to thank you personally—I was wondering if you'd care for two passes to the Rex Theatre? There is a wonderful picture playing.'

Milly beamed back at her. 'Thank you Mrs Anderson—I've already seen that picture, but it is most kind of you.'

'Are you fond of flowers, perhaps?'

'Oh I *do* so love daffodils, Mrs Anderson!'

'Wonderful!' Ethel exclaimed, clasping her hands in delight. 'My husband will bring you a bunch. I'm just dropping the boys at school, could I possibly call in on the way past this afternoon and gather a few more items on my way home?'

'Certainly Mrs Anderson, that will be no problem,' Milly replied, as Ethel ushered her boys towards the door.

———•———

One day there was a loud knock at the front door. Ethel opened it to find a big, burly man standing there.

'Lady Betty Anderson?' he demanded, before shoving an envelope towards her and turning on his heels.

She owed another car hire company over £10 (over $1000) and they were taking her to court.

The little family moved the next day to a smaller house further away from the beach. Ethel didn't appear in court, and in her absence was fined nearly £30 and given two days to pay.

The boys returned to their new home from school one day to find their mother wasn't there. This was not unusual, so they looked in the cupboards—nothing much to eat—and no sixpence on the table, so she wouldn't be gone too long. But hours turned into a day, two days, three . . . no mother, nothing to eat. Finally the neighbours realised something was amiss and took them in for a feed, sharing the little they had with two more hungry mouths.

The next morning came a knock on the door. Thinking it was Ethel, the boys opened the door, but it wasn't their mother; standing there instead was a police officer and a man from the Child Welfare Department. They scooped the bewildered boys up like a couple of stray cats and placed them into a boys' institution, after which Frank and Basil were soon separated.

All they wanted was for their mother to whisk them away, but she couldn't—she was in way too much trouble.

14

THE DRAPERY AFFAIR &
NURSE FLORENCE ANDERSON

While the boys were at school, Ethel had been arrested at their new home.

It was November 1933. Ethel was starting to carry a lot of weight by now, and with her fine clothes, jewellery and posh manner had been able to play the well-to-do matron convincingly. Tell them what you think they want to hear and pander to their desires: it had certainly worked well for her in the past.

But she was also coming to the attention of the police in South Australia—she'd been plying her trade too successfully for too long in one place, opening many accounts under the names of Anderson and Gardiner.

The previous month, she'd gone to a drapery store, Coles & Hughes, to buy some soft furnishings—curtains, rugs, cushions—for their new home. Ethel had told the manager,

Mr Eric Thompson, that she was Mrs Gardiner, wife of a large station owner from New South Wales. They had taken a house in Henley Beach for a few months as her husband had had a nervous breakdown, and they were in South Australia to take in the sea air and give him time to recover. The house was partly furnished, she casually told the manager as she walked around fingering the fine fabrics, but they were in need of some quality drapery to make it feel like home. She then asked whether it would be convenient for her to open an account.

Mr Thompson politely explained that they didn't make many accounts, especially with the effects of the Depression still being felt. Things were so bad, he confided, that he was concerned for his own job.

She looked at him with concern. 'Do you do business with Sargood Gardiner of Melbourne and Sydney, perhaps?' she asked, naming a big importer of drapery.

'A little, Mrs Gardiner,' Mr Thompson replied.

'Well, my husband is also a part owner in the firm,' Ethel stated confidently.

With that, Mr Thompson led her to one of his assistants and said it would be fine to supply Mrs Gardiner with goods, but made a point of advising Ethel that the account would have to be settled by the first day of the following month.

On the first of November, Mr Thompson received a letter from Ethel asking to meet her the following morning at a fashionable hotel in Adelaide. When he arrived, he found her sitting in the lounge, waiting. She stood and greeted him with a smile before motioning towards the chair opposite.

'I expect you wonder why I wish to see you?' she asked, after they sat down. He said that he did, and handed her the outstanding account.

'I will take this home and check it against my dockets,' she said thoughtfully, looking down at the bill. 'I'll get my husband to write out a cheque for the, uh, £7 13s 10d, tomorrow,' she added, before folding the docket and carefully placing it in her handbag.

'I have been thinking of all your trouble,' Ethel explained. 'I feel that I would like to make you very happy.' She paused and looked at him carefully. 'Are you duty-bound to stay in Australia?'

'No,' he replied slowly.

'If I offered you £1000 and a shop in New Zealand, would you care to go and start in business on your own?'

'Why do you make this offer to me?' a stunned Mr Thompson asked in return.

'Because I think you are an honest man, and I would like to make you happy.'

He stared at her in disbelief. 'What do you expect in return?'

'I expect nothing in return, only to see you happy,' Ethel replied sweetly.

Mr Thompson sat back against his chair, folding his arms against his chest, and looked thoughtfully at her.

Fearing she was losing the advantage, Ethel brought out one of her favourite stories, with a few variations.

'My father is a director of a large cotton factory in England,' she began, 'and my mother is one of the Coats, a cousin of Coats—you know, the cotton people,' she explained.

Mr Thompson nodded his head slowly in understanding as she continued on. 'If I offered you your expenses to England and guaranteed you a position with my father for two years, would you accept it?'

'Why do you offer this to me?' he asked again in bewilderment.

'Because I like you,' was Ethel's simple explanation.

'But why would your father hire me? He doesn't know me and there are *millions* of people out of work now,' he persisted.

Ethel smiled and tried again. 'I could settle you with £5000 on your arrival in England.'

Mr Thompson seemed confused as he pondered her proposal. He looked at his watch and asked if she would like lunch, and Ethel readily agreed. He paid for an expensive cocktail to start with, and they continued talking throughout the meal before retiring back to the lounge to finish their conversation.

Ethel sat in her chair and smiled at Mr Thompson, leant forward and placed her hand gently on his leg. She smiled to herself when she saw his eyes dwell on her exposed cleavage as she leant in close. 'Eric—is it alright if I call you Eric?' she asked.

Mr Thompson pulled his eyes away from her cleavage to her smiling face.

'I will be honest with you,' she began. 'My husband is a sick man and it is out of duty that I have accompanied him here to South Australia, but we have been unhappy for some time, and no longer sleep together as man and wife,' she sighed. 'My time is my own,' she added confidently, fixing him with her bright blue eyes. 'I could see you whenever you would like.'

Mr Thompson gently pulled his leg away from her hand and sat himself upright. 'I am sorry Mrs Anderson if you have mistaken me in some way, but I am engaged to be married!'

With exaggerated modesty, Ethel placed her hands into her lap and gave the drapery manager a small smile. 'No need to apologise Mr Thompson,' she said as if nothing intimate had taken place between them.

She pulled her shoulders back and smiled sweetly at him. 'May I suggest we meet again tomorrow to discuss your trip to England?'

A relieved Mr Thompson agreed—but the next day when she didn't show up, he went straight to the police. He told them he could not get the gist of the woman. He thought she was a most unusual lady, spellbinding; he had wanted to believe what she had been telling him, but couldn't quite.

———

Ethel was furious when she was arrested. Mr Thompson had fabricated the entire tale, she insisted. She was so caught up in her fight for innocence that she failed to mention to anyone the fact that her boys were fending for themselves. She was convinced she would be let out before the case went to trial. Ethel demanded the case be brought before a jury so she could state her side of the story to those who would listen and understand her plight. She was innocent! At her preliminary hearing, she was placed on a 50-pound bond and allowed to go home until her next court appearance in front of a jury, only to be told by the neighbours that her boys had been collected by Child Welfare. She would go to the orphanage and find them, after the trial was over; she had too much on her hands already. Unfortunately for Ethel, Mr Thompson was not the only witness at the trial. Ethel had also had a conversation with an assistant at the Coles & Hughes store, Lizzie Clemson, whose husband had been out of work for some time. Lizzie had confided in Ethel that she and her husband were looking for a married couple's job; Ethel gleefully replied that her husband owned a big station in Queensland, and would get the two of them a position there. It was Lizzie's testimony that ended the second day of the trial. Ethel had fabricated a different state for her husband's station in her conversation with Lizzie and was exposed in court as an opportunistic liar by Mr. J.P. Walsh the prosecuting lawyer. Because she had insisted on a trial by jury in a higher court, she genuinely feared a gaol sentence, especially if the police happened to find out about the rest of her misdemeanours.

For just under a year now, Ethel had been talking her way in and out of jewellery stores, clothing shops and car hire companies in and around Adelaide, mainly using the names Gardiner and Anderson, but also McEwan, Stevens and Lockwood as well, and even posing as a military wife, Mrs Colonel Smith, at one store. She needed to get out of South Australia fast, before the police connected all the dots.

On the third day of her trial at the Criminal Court, Ethel's name was read out three times inside and outside the courtroom, but she was nowhere to be found. She lost the £50 bond she'd had to put up before being let out on bail, together with her cheque book for the account her father paid her allowance into, and her passport; everything was in police custody.

That morning, Ethel had seen an advertisement in the *Advertiser* for a position as a home nurse for an elderly lady, Mrs Catherine Hunt, who lived in the town of Wolseley, eight miles from the Victorian/South Australian border.

Ethel attended the home of Mrs Hunt's daughter in Adelaide for an interview, removing her pearls and earrings beforehand.

'Thank you for coming, Nurse Anderson,' the good lady said. 'We are in need of a nurse for my mother, who has become quite frail in the last few weeks.'

'So I understand,' Ethel replied politely. 'As I mentioned on the telephone, I was a nurse in the Great War and saw much suffering,' she began. 'And I have looked after many patients in their own homes over the years since the end of that dreadful time,' she added. 'Caring for others is my calling.'

'You have no family, I understand?' the daughter asked.

'No, I was married at the start of the war, but my husband, a captain in the army, was killed on the Somme,' Ethel explained. 'I threw myself into my work in my grief,' she said, letting out a large sigh. 'I think my patients have become my family ever since.'

'You understand there are some domestic duties as well as nursing duties?' the daughter asked eagerly.

'Yes, that doesn't concern me,' Ethel remarked with a re-assuring smile, 'as long as my patient is well cared for.' Cleaning was the least of her worries.

'My mother lives in quite a small country town; I hope that doesn't concern you Florence—may I call you Florence?' the daughter asked hurriedly.

'Of course,' Ethel replied. 'And I don't mind a little country town at all,' she confirmed. 'I prefer a more sedate life.'

———

Ethel's stints as a former World War I nurse were always the same: for a short duration, and for her own financial advantage.

Ethel worked for Mrs Hunt for a total of nine days. She then took her wages—as well as a gold ring, a gold and ruby brooch, and five pounds in bank notes from the old lady—and quietly slipped across the Victorian border.

15

MISS HORDERN

Ethel next found herself in the goldmining town of Ballarat, where she checked into a top-class boarding house. Boarding houses were common enough back then, often cheaper than a hotel and usually for a longer term; they were often set up in large old houses converted into separate rooms. She told the landlady that she was the daughter of the wealthy Sydney identity Sir Samuel Hordern, and was having a look around the district for a holiday house for her family to purchase.

Ethel couldn't believe how lovely the people in the country community were, happily lending her money on account, taking on her story with delight—but it was also this openness that was her undoing. In less than a week, the florist who supplied her with fresh flowers daily had shared her version of the lovely Miss Hordern's story to the milliner—namely that the rich lady had been a nurse in the Great War on the Western Front.

The milliner was certain the florist must have been mistaken, as her charming new rich client told her she had worked for the War Office and travelled incognito to the Continent. The milliner was delighted at having sold an expensive black crocodile-skin handbag to such an esteemed person and was looking forward to receiving the funds from Sir Hordern himself when he arrived in the town. And besides, she liked the War Office story: not only was Miss Hordern rich and charming, she had also been a daring spy.

Annoyed that the milliner was calling her mistaken, the florist confronted Miss Hordern when she passed by her shop the next morning. Ethel assured the florist it was in fact her friend the milliner who had the facts wrong, then immediately set about leaving town—owing money to the boarding house, the florist, the taxi driver, the hairdresser and the milliner. Ethel learnt her lesson: stick to one story in a country town.

Next stop, Melbourne, where Ethel was at a loose end, having no identity papers and no money coming to her from her father. Her real father, unaware of her situation, would be sending money into her account, but the Adelaide police had her cheque book.

She'd heard about Perth, the capital city of the enormous state of Western Australia. Remote and isolated, Perth was a new town, a new part of the world she hadn't been to.

She'd go and see what it was like.

———•———

At Port Melbourne, Ethel asked the booking clerk how much the fare was to Perth. She was in luck, the clerk informed her— there was a ship leaving that very afternoon.

Ethel didn't have the money for the first-class fare, but was determined not to travel in any other fashion. She turned and watched as a vice-regal party made its way into the departure lounge, waiting to board the SS *Orsova* for Fremantle. She started chatting with a young man on the edge of the group. She introduced herself to him as the English opera singer Eva Turner—wearing her expensive jewellery, fine clothes and clutching her smart crocodile-skin handbag, she certainly looked the part. With all the charm she could muster, Ethel made her way on board with the Governor-General and his entourage.

Once safely on board, Ethel settled down on the promenade deck and waited until the bell rang for all the visitors to leave. She found what she thought looked like an empty cabin, then made her way into the lounge and ordered herself a cocktail as the boat left the harbour.

Ethel had travelled on enough boats to know who was who, so she told the purser that her name must have been missed on the ship's manifest. She was a famous English opera singer, travelling with the Governor-General, whose booking had been misplaced. Tell people what they want to hear, was her motto, after all, and she had no trouble persuading the purser that first class was where she belonged.

When the young man Ethel had initially introduced herself to asked her to sing for them after dinner, she informed her companions at the dinner table that she was resting her vocal chords due to a recent infection, and as much as she would have loved to give them a rendition from *Aida*, she couldn't possibly risk damaging her livelihood, and again they seemed to believe her.

When the boat arrived in Fremantle, she was even given a ride into the State Theatre with the Governor-General, but Ethel couldn't find much of interest in Perth, considering it little more than a dusty country town. She sold Mrs Hunt's brooch and, not finding a ship heading back to the eastern states, decided to catch the train back to Adelaide. She'd heard the trip was luxurious, but she was bored and unimpressed by the dismal array of passengers—no class, no lively conversation to be had—and mile upon mile of empty desert.

From Adelaide, she quickly caught a train to Melbourne, not wanting to stay in the state where she was still a wanted woman.

16

MRS ANN DERSON

Ethel made her way to Melbourne's eastern suburbs, and went to work.

Again using her movie star name Gloria Grey she plied her trade in only the best establishments, cashing cheques from a bank account she had opened with only one pound, and obtaining numerous luxury items.

When things got a bit hot in Melbourne, she dyed her hair a different shade and travelled up to Sydney.

Under the various names of Florence Dunkley, Elizabeth Gardner, Elizabeth Anderson, Elizabeth King, Lady Betty Anderson, Ann Derson, Florence Derson, Gloria Grey and Pamela Pilkington she took Sydney by storm, passing valueless cheques, from the city to Ryde and the quieter northern beach suburbs—all new areas for her. She even managed to convince one gullible jeweller that she was Mrs Fingleton, the wife of a member of the Australian Cricket Team; he happily gave her a large cameo brooch on credit, never to see the delightful cricketer's wife, or brooch, again.

After a close call with one shop owner who didn't quite believe one of her stories, Ethel decided to head back to Melbourne. She'd learnt to keep on the move.

But she hadn't quite learnt how to keep out of trouble. Stopping for a few days in the affluent wool town of Goulburn, about 120 miles from Sydney, she was arrested for evading taxi fares, under the name Gloria Grey; not known in New South Wales under that name, she was granted bail, but immediately absconded on the Sydney to Melbourne train and continued her journey south.

Another of her other popular aliases at the time was Judith Anderson. The real Judith Anderson was 36, born in Adelaide seven months before Ethel's actual birthday, and had been working on the stage in Britain opposite the likes of Laurence Olivier, one of Ethel's favourite leading men. According to the yellow press accounts that Ethel loved to read, the actress was planning on moving to Hollywood to break into the movies, and was the Aussie golden star of the moment. She suited Ethel well.

As Judith, she stopped at Albury on the Victorian/New South Wales border, where she managed to cash a cheque for twenty pounds ($1000) with a shopkeeper named Mary Walsh. She loved the thrill of obtaining goods and money from unsuspecting people—and if she'd performed the con well enough the shopkeepers would be too embarrassed to tell the police. But she was getting greedy.

Her most successful method at that time was to waltz into a classy shop and casually mention that she mixed in only the best social circles, and that she would bring these people into their shop to buy an item or two. Through these means she procured countless pricey items for free and on account, and managed to cash worthless cheques, before disappearing once more.

But within days of arriving back in Melbourne, Ethel was recognised by a saleswoman who she'd conned when working at another store, and was quickly picked up by police.

———–·—————

Ethel was headed back into the court system, this time in Victoria, with 25 different charges of acting under false pretences against her. It seemed there were at least 25 people in Victoria who weren't too embarrassed to tell the police about how they'd been duped.

It eventually became known to the Victorian police that Ethel had absconded on bail from South Australia during the Coles & Hughes drapery case the year before—but with 25 charges against her in Victoria, the South Australian police felt it wasn't worth their while bringing her back to South Australia to face the older charges; the Victorians could deal with her.

The case was heard in the first week of June 1934, with Florence Elizabeth Ethel Anderson, 36, being charged under the name of Gloria Grey.

Through her lawyer, Severin Zichy-Woinarski, Ethel's usual half-fanciful tales emerged. He told the court that she had been buffeted by fate and betrayed by a man. She had been a nurse in the war and married an army captain who was killed shortly afterwards. She had then married again and had two children, but her new husband had deserted her and returned to his home country, Australia. She followed him out with their children, only to find he was a bigamist; he then blackmailed her, saying she had known she was party to a bigamous marriage, and demanding she pay him money to keep quiet. (Perhaps this blackmail ploy was one that Ethel herself had used over the years to extract more sums of money from unsuspecting men.)

After laying down the foundations of her story, her lawyer tried to turn the blame onto the shopkeepers, telling the judge that they should expect little sympathy from the court. These tradespeople were as much to blame for having given her credit as she was for having passed bad cheques.

The judge—who also happened to be Mr Zichy-Woinarski's father—agreed, saying he never ceased to wonder at the credulity of tradespeople in the city, who accepted good appearances and manners, and who were ready to give credit and cash cheques without first making proper enquiry. He thought they were to blame for their credulity, but qualified this by saying he did not think they should be exploited.

Ethel was found guilty of ten of the original 25 charges, and sentenced to six months in gaol. She was off to prison, again.

Good thing the judge didn't know about all those cases in New South Wales.

17

MISS TURNER

By the time Ethel had served six hard months in Pentridge Prison, she'd had enough of Victoria, and again headed north to Sydney. She needed to get away before the South Australian system caught up with her.

Ethel left gaol with a limp, a result of a disagreement with a fellow prisoner that would give her arthritis in her left leg in later years. She had, however, also gleaned some useful information from her fellow inmates that would serve her well.

She wanted to get back to England, but first she needed funds.

She travelled up to New South Wales, and in three weeks took three more unsuspecting men to the cleaners, working again as Nurse Florence Anderson, the Great War nurse looking after the elderly and sick at home. Within days of arriving and telling her stories of woe, she was gone again, with their cash.

Ethel was always on the lookout for ways to move on and better herself. For weeks the newspapers had been filled with the exciting news that the Australian cricket team and the Davis Cup tennis team would be travelling together on the RMS *Orford* to England for the European summer. With memories of being the fictitious Mrs Fingleton, and fantasies about even possibly becoming her, Ethel wanted to be on that boat to England. She wasn't alone: everyone who could afford a ticket wanted to be there—though Ethel of course didn't plan on buying a ticket.

She fronted up to Sydney Harbour and boarded the enormous liner with all the other visitors and travellers, expecting to rub shoulders with some of the famous sportspeople and wealthy travellers, only to find that the teams were boarding in the next ports of Melbourne and Perth. No matter; she'd meet them then.

As the ship's bell rang, warning visitors to return to the dock, Ethel moved to the lounge and was about to order a drink when a smartly dressed ship's officer asked her for her name and cabin number. With the ship completely full, and with so much interest in the cricket and tennis players, they were checking everyone left on board.

Ethel tried to charm him, to no avail. He demanded to know her cabin number, and upon checking the passenger list promptly turfed her off the ship.

Fuming, she stood in the international departures terminal and watched through the large glass windows as the gangplank was removed from the *Orford* and passengers threw paper streamers to friends and relatives far below. The side of the ship looked like a colourful wedding veil billowing in the wind, with each streamer flying upwards as it broke or was pulled from a wellwisher's hand as the ship left port.

Ethel turned and strolled over to a shipping clerk and asked where the next ship coming into the port was heading.

He looked through his notes, then looked up. 'It is the *Niagara*, heading for San Francisco.'

'When will it be arriving?' she asked casually.

'Tomorrow morning, leaving Thursday. Were you after a ticket?'

'No thank you, I was just curious,' she replied, then slowly made her way from the port.

San Francisco? Why not.

———•••———

That Thursday Ethel arrived three hours before departure and made her way onto the RMS *Niagara*. She couldn't find a free berth anywhere, so she hid her bag in a lifeboat and settled into the lounge as the ship departed.

She started up several conversations with various people and settled on one man who seemed to be travelling alone, Mr Frank Leitch.

'My father's name is Frank!' she exclaimed in delight, when he told her his name.

'And I'm sorry, your name . . .'

'Oh, how silly of me—we haven't been formally introduced,' Ethel gushed. 'My name is Eva Turner, Miss Eva Turner.'

'And what brings you on this journey, Miss Turner?' he asked conversationally.

'I've always wanted to see the West Coast of America. I have travelled extensively since the war, but haven't as yet explored that side of the country,' she remarked, enjoying how her story was progressing. 'I may go across to New York before heading home though—I *so* love New York.'

'And home would be?'

'Why, the United Kingdom,' she replied in her best plummy tones. 'My father works in the family business there, cotton,' she said smugly, warming to one of her usual themes. Their conversation continued, Ethel being as charming as she could be, hoping to get herself a berth for the night.

Mr Leitch told her he was travelling to New Zealand on family business, and he took great pains to point out that he was in fact married—*happily* married—when Ethel's attentions became rather more personal than he was comfortable with. He bid her goodnight at the end of the evening and wished her an enjoyable voyage.

Ethel sat back in her chair, dejected. Was she losing her touch? Where was she going to spend the night? The room was emptying and the wait staff were clearing up after the last of the guests. She made her way out towards the lifeboat where she'd hidden her bag, and noticed the tonneau latching she had loosened to place her bag inside was firmly back in place—did she have the right one?

'You lookin' for some'n?' asked a thickly accented Scottish voice. Ethel turned to see a burly silhouette against the cabin lights.

'No, no . . . I thought I'd just go for a stroll before retiring,' she answered, then went to walk away.

He stepped in front of her.

'Yer sure?' he asked, holding up her bag.

———·—·———

The shipping company decided not to turn the boat around, instead sending a telegram notifying Sydney Harbour of a stowaway.

To her horror, they hid the buxom Miss Turner in the dark hold for the two days and night it took to reach Auckland. Even then they kept her down in the hold for what seemed like hours, until all the passengers had finally disembarked and were long gone.

She heard the lock being opened in the solid steel door and turned to face it. There standing in the doorway was her captor.

'Ah, Mr McKenzie, so lovely to see you again!' Ethel said with more gaiety than she certainly felt.

'Miss Turner,' the Scot said. 'Will yer come with me please.'

'Certainly Mr McKenzie,' said Ethel, picking up her small black hat and placing it on the back of her head with care. 'I must look a fright!'

'Won't matter where *yer* going,' she heard the third mate scoff.

'Come on Miss Turner, we don't have all day,' urged Mr McKenzie, making his way to the steel steps leading up out of the hold.

She followed closely as he led her up onto the deck. There stood the Captain who had grilled her the morning after she'd been found, standing with her bag at his feet, two New Zealand police officers standing next to him.

'Captain, so lovely to see you again,' Ethel said breezily.

'This is her,' the captain said. The officers immediately came up on either side of her, one grabbing her arm roughly. Ethel glared at him and tried to pull herself into a more dignified pose.

'She doesn't seem to have any papers or passport on her, but she says her name is Turner,' the captain told them.

Ethel was staring at the captain with her big blue eyes. Then he turned to leave.

'Thank you captain,' she said, pulling her shoulders back, lifting her chin slightly. 'It has been an *interesting* cruise!'

'Come on you,' said the officer holding her arm, pulling her towards the gangway.

Ethel followed, but still looking at the captain, had one last thing to say:

'I will NOT be recommending your ship to my friends.'

Behind her, McKenzie gave a short laugh as she was led away.

'What a dame!'

The shipping company decided not to prosecute Ethel. Instead it sent her back to Sydney on the next liner out, the *Monowai*. As she was led off the ship, she was met by members of the press; her stowaway story had caught their attention.

'Good afternoon, gentlemen,' she greeted them, as the sailor who had escorted her off the ship scurried back up the gangway.

'Miss Turner,' one reporter asked eagerly, 'how did you get on board?'

'I did it vice-regal fashion,' Ethel replied with a wave of her hand. 'I followed an official-looking party on board, and just stayed.' Which wasn't true of course; she was retelling her previous trip from a few months before.

'Where are you from, Miss Turner?' another young reporter asked impatiently.

'I came up from South Australia, I travelled to Sydney looking for work, and love the idea of working at sea,' she said almost dreamily. 'I love the sea, I have a craving for sea life—if I had been a man I would have been a sea captain.' She was enjoying herself immensely, watching them scribbling down her every word on their notepads.

'I journeyed as far as Fremantle last year and was not detected,' she added for effect, pausing and making sure all eyes were back on her. 'And I planned to stow away on the *Orford*, on which the Australian cricketers are travelling, but was found and escorted off before it left port,' she watched them scratch her words into their pads.

'I then joined an interstate passenger vessel for Melbourne and travelled undetected, and made a second attempt to board the *Orford*, but failed, so when I saw the *Niagara* heading to the United States of America, I thought I would go and see the world,' she declared, exaggerating her story with an additional journey. She paused as the assembled reporters, soaking it up, recorded every word she was saying.

'Miss Turner,' the first reported asked, 'how were you treated?'

'Dreadfully!' she replied. 'I was imprisoned in the ship's locker for the trip back here, and on the *Niagara* they threw me down in a dark hold for days and nights—it was frightful! And then when I arrived in New Zealand, the police insisted I be taken ashore and I had to spend several nights with the Salvation Army!' Ethel really was enjoying how much they were hanging off every word. 'The police in New Zealand treated me shockingly—not nearly as considerate as the Australian police.'

'You've been in trouble with the law before?' the second reporter asked eagerly.

'No, no, of course not—only when I was escorted off the *Orford*,' she replied hurriedly. 'Now if you will excuse me I need to make arrangements.'

Ethel pushed her way through the reporters as quickly as she could and, holding her bag tightly, caught a taxi at the international terminal exit.

18

LADY BETTY BALFOUR

February 1935 and Ethel was back in Sydney, but keeping on the move. Using her old ruse of bouncing cheques, she conned one shopkeeper for £4 (just over $400), then headed to the southern beach suburb of Cronulla, where she once again became the returned servicewoman Nurse Anderson. There she looked after two more World War I veterans, Tasman Joseph Ward and William Carmody, and in the space of a week had taken a combined sum of £10 in cash from them.

Next she again headed north to Brisbane and started living with a man called Mr Balfour. She began calling herself Betty Balfour, or Lady Betty Balfour, both famous people at the time. Betty Balfour was an English screen actress who came to fame in the silent movie era and was known as 'Britain's Queen of Happiness' by her fans. The real Lady Elizabeth Edith 'Betty' Balfour was married to Gerald Balfour, Second Earl of Balfour, and brother of the British conservative Prime Minister Arthur Balfour.

Ethel could see herself as both a movie star and a member of the peerage, so it seemed only right for her to live her new life as Betty.

Unfortunately for Ethel, Mr Balfour was no gentleman, and when he struck her she decided it was time to move on—taking his trusty cheque book with her, and some money from a kindly neighbour who, after hearing one of Ethel's sob stories about her abusive husband Mr Balfour, happily lent her the money to cover her medical bills.

Over the next few days she swindled some more Brisbane shopkeepers with Mr Balfour's cheques. It was becoming harder to open cheque accounts without identification papers, so each cheque she had left became precious.

She made her way back down to Victoria, where she made contact with a former inmate from Pentridge, who gave Ethel the name and address of a corrupt Justice of the Peace—let's call him 'Mr Peace'—who might be willing to help her get a fake birth certificate so she could apply for a passport to England.

Mr Peace's office turned out to be a run-down chemist shop in a working-class suburb to the north of Melbourne. The effects of the Depression were still obvious in the area, with many shops boarded up on the busy road out of the city.

Ethel entered the chemist with some unease.

'I'm here to see Mr Peace,' she stated to the young man who came to serve her.

'Was it medical?' the man asked tentatively, looking her up and down curiously. With her fur-lined black jacket, lustrous pearls and neat appearance, she looked out of place in the dark, drab shop.

'No, something else,' Ethel replied, trying to sound confident.

She needn't have worried. The assistant nodded knowingly and motioned for her to follow him. They walked along a short hallway; he knocked on a door towards the end of it, and then opened it without waiting for a reply. The assistant looked at Ethel and stood back to let her bulk through.

Her eyes had to adjust to the darkened room, but she saw a stooped man rise from his chair behind a desk. 'Mr Peace?' she asked, and saw the old man stand and smile at her through the gloom.

'Yes my dear, can I help you?' he asked, indicating a wooden chair opposite him. Ethel made her way towards it, brushed it off and eased herself down as Mr Peace too returned to his seat.

'I am after some documentation, and I was reliably informed you may be able to help me.'

'I see,' he said looking at her carefully. 'May I ask who gave you that information?'

Ethel mentioned the name of her fellow former inmate and the man smiled at her. 'Yes of course. Now, did she mention a fee?' he asked.

Ethel nodded and watched as he turned around to pull some documents out of a cupboard behind him. He squinted at them in the dim light coming in through the dirty window, in a way that made her think he looked like a hunched mole, then watched as he made his way around the desk to sit alongside her.

'Now, what proof of identification do you have?' he asked, turning to her.

She looked at him in surprise. 'Well, nothing I can use,' she replied.

'Ah then,' he said smiling sadly. 'That is difficult.'

They looked at each other in silence, before Ethel finally asked quietly, 'You cannot help me?'

'I did not say that my dear—it will just cost you a little more.'

Ethel regarded him suspiciously. 'How much more?'

'Let us see what we have and I'll let you know,' he replied. 'Your name?'

'Betty Balfour,' she replied, lifting her head, and saw his eyebrows raise.

'Really?' he asked.

She stared at him for a moment in defiance, then reluctantly admitted it wasn't her real name. He nodded slowly, then cleared his throat. 'Well then my dear, I'm afraid I will have to charge accordingly. I gather there would be some urgency to this application as well?'

Ethel replied with a nod and asked, 'How much?'

'What do you require?'

'A birth certificate,' she replied quickly. 'And, a passport.' Any documentation she had previously had been left behind in Adelaide when she absconded.

Mr Peace nodded and contemplated her for a moment. 'Fifty pounds,' he announced.

Ethel grasped her throat dramatically. 'I can't afford that!' she whispered, thinking of her first-class fare back to England.

'Well then my dear, I cannot help you,' he said, shuffling his papers in front of him and about to rise from his seat.

Ethel's hand shot out and held his upper leg. 'Is there not some way I could make it worth your while?' she asked.

He took a moment to assess the large, elegantly dressed woman beside him. 'I am afraid, my dear, that at my age, cash is more important.'

Ethel removed her hand and contemplated the Justice of the Peace beside her. She wanted to get out of Australia, and he seemed the only way to get a passport or any form of identification. She didn't want to stow away on a ship again, and she couldn't open another bank account, fictitious or otherwise, without any identification.

'I will have the money,' she replied.

Mr Peace gave her a broad smile, picked up his fountain pen and started looking through the documents before him.

'Now then, my dear, what name would you like?'

19

MISS HARVEY

Pamela Judith Eve Harvey arrived in the New Zealand capital of Wellington in the summer of 1935. She had chosen the names of four different movie stars and combined them to produce her new alias.

Pamela Brown was an up-and-coming English movie star, and Ethel liked the name Pamela, it had a nice modern ring to it. Judith she kept from her alias Judith Anderson, which had worked so well for her, and she chose Eve after reading an article about an American actress, Eve Arden, who had created her stage name from two cosmetic bottles on her dressing room table: Evening in Paris and another by Elizabeth Arden. (Like Ethel, movie stars *also* chose names they could relate to—she liked that!) Her new surname was from another favourite movie star, Lilian Harvey, who had been a successful silent movie star and was now a famous talkie star.

Ethel's new name was complete: Pamela Judith Eve Harvey, known to her friends as Eve.

She had also shaved nine years off her age: Miss Eve Harvey was now 29 years old.

Mr Peace's fee had meant she couldn't afford to go all the way back to Britain first class, so she decided she'd travel a little closer by until things cooled down. Her new passport was duly issued, for a new life, in a new country.

———·••·———

On the ship to Wellington, Ethel befriended Mr and Mrs MacTaggert, telling them how she was an artist, a wealthy woman of means with relatives in the cotton trade, travelling on a world tour, and eager to explore the country of New Zealand.

Mrs MacTaggert seemed surprised when she learnt her new friend's age, but Ethel tried not to appear too mortified and explained that she had suffered greatly over the years, losing her mother as a baby and having nursed her elderly father for many years, and perhaps that was why she looked a little older than she was.

Mr MacTaggert was a middle-aged civil engineer heading to an international engineers conference in Wellington, and when it was realised that their new friend Miss Harvey had no fixed plans and no acquaintances in the new country, they suggested she stay and explore Wellington with them for a few days, especially as Mr MacTaggert would be at the conference during the days.

So Ethel joined the MacTaggerts as they left the ship at Waterloo Quay and caught a taxi with them to the Hotel St George, an impressive Art Deco hotel where the conference was to be held. At the front desk, Mr MacTaggert enquired about a room for Miss Harvey, and was informed the hotel was fully booked.

'Come now man,' Mr MacTaggert said to the concierge, 'you must keep a room or two spare—it is important that Miss Harvey here is properly accommodated.'

'I was so looking forward to staying at your establishment!' Ethel gushed. 'I had heard so many wonderful things from your ambassador Sir Thomas Wilford back home in England,' she lied. 'I should have booked *weeks* ago, but it was a spur of the moment decision to come now rather than in the autumn.' The concierge took in Ethel's fine clothing, her regal demeanour and prim, posh voice, while Ethel looked at him as sweetly as she could.

'I do have a small room that—' the concierge began.

'Oh wonderful! I hope I haven't put you out at all,' Ethel immediately exclaimed, in her plummiest of tones. 'I was hoping to stay with my friends here,' she said, beaming at the impressed Mrs MacTaggert, before turning back to the concierge. 'I will have to tell Sir Thomas what a wonderful fellow you are.' The concierge smiled and asked her to fill in the register, and she was in.

That night at dinner, the engineers and their wives met for drinks in the lounge and Mr MacTaggert formally introduced Ethel to the guest speaker, Mr William Coradine. At 55, he was sixteen years older than Ethel, and 25 years older than her alias Eve. A single civil engineer, he had recently sold his share of a Ceylon tea plantation and was heading back to Britain to undertake some consultative work at Whitehall before officially retiring.

William Alexander Coradine was too good an opportunity to miss.

20

MRS CORADINE

William Coradine had planned to attend the engineers conference, taking the opportunity to visit his uncle James Coradine,
who he had never met, and his large extended family, before
returning to a sedate life of semi-retirement back in England.
But then he met Ethel.

Eve explored Wellington by day with her new friend Mrs
McTaggart and some of the other wives at the conference, and
as the only unaccompanied lady in their group, managed to
escort the single Mr Coradine to all the official functions over
the week-long conference.

Ethel used all of her considerable charm to snaffle the rich,
middle-aged colonial, travelling with him after the conference, with a couple from Ceylon, to visit his uncle James.
William seemed delighted to be of interest to such a delightful young woman. He told her all about his life and she was

fascinated. He was the son of a strict Methodist preacher; his mother had died when he was young, and he and his father had travelled to Ceylon as missionaries for six years. When they returned his father remarried and William had several younger siblings, but he didn't know them very well as he had been shipped off to public school in Norfolk, near his father's new parish. He trained as a civil engineer when he had finished school, and after working in London for a few years took a job in the city of Kandy in central Ceylon, and eventually became an investor in a large tea plantation, living the life of a Ceylonese colonial. Now, he was ready to return to England, having accepted a job at Whitehall; he had sold his stake in the plantation and was heading back, via New Zealand, a very wealthy bachelor.

Once again Ethel had a chance at a life free from deception, relatively speaking. She could be who she was meant to be.

She told him her father had been a doctor in Harley Street, but had died two years before she embarked on her world trip, and she had nursed him through a long, horrible illness. Her mother, a member of the Coats cotton dynasty, had also died when she was quite young, so they had something in common. She had never married, or had any children, but now she was heading back to England, and felt she could possibly settle down, if he was interested.

Mr Coradine was delighted, and on 27 February 1935 they were married at his uncle's parish church in Rotorua. With a fresh marriage certificate, Eve Coradine, née Harvey, applied for a new passport for her new life. While they waited for the passport to be processed, the newlyweds spent the next few months on an extended honeymoon, travelling throughout New Zealand and visiting the remote and dramatic Milford Sound.

They set off for England as a bitter winter was descending upon Wellington, travelling first class on the SS *Remuera*. The only notable event that interrupted Ethel's partying was the death of an elderly woman in third class, who was buried at sea with much ceremony, her white sheet-sheathed body slipping beneath the waves.

Arriving in Southampton in July 1935, the Coradines found a home in fashionable Chelsea, and William worked as a Crown Agent for the Colonies at Whitehall, frequently spoiling his new wife with cash and gifts. Ethel was content: she was invited to all the best Chelsea social occasions, had a rich, respectable husband, a beautiful home she could entertain in freely—and then life took an unexpected turn. At nearly 40 years of age, she found out she was pregnant.

William was ecstatic; he was going to be a father. Ethel was not nearly as excited. She carried the child around reluctantly, feeling every bit her age, and complained to her indulgent husband at every opportunity.

Ethel Mary Coradine arrived on 22 September 1936, leaving Ethel with complications that would plague her for years to come.

She was a lovely baby, and the nanny they hired was attentive, but when she was just two weeks old, she went to sleep quite normally one night and never woke up.

Mr Coradine was heartbroken. Filled with grief, his health and spirits deteriorated, and he officially retired. Ethel wanted to sell the house, saying it was filled with sad memories, and that they should move somewhere more gay and start again, but all William wanted to do was stay indoors and mourn.

———·——

So, Ethel took off, to the French Riviera. She had always wanted to live in the playground of the rich and famous that she had seen again and again portrayed on film.

It was a turbulent time, with the Spanish Civil War casting long shadows over Europe, and in England rumblings of another Great War as King Edward VIII abdicated and married Mrs Wallis Simpson in France in June 1937, and it was reported that they were holidaying in the French Riviera. With the added bonus of scandalous royalty in the area, Ethel wanted a piece of that action.

On arriving in Nice in November 1937, Ethel excitedly settled into a fashionable hotel overlooking the promenade across the Bay of Angels, aiming to get in with 'the set'. The Côte d'Azur was luxurious, dazzling and filled with beautiful people—certainly a far more glamorous version of Henley Beach, St Kilda or Blackpool.

Ethel dolled herself up and lorded herself about town, trying to get invites with anyone of note. Not succeeding, she watched in frustration as those she most wanted to be seen with emerged from their extensive villas and châteaux with sweeping gardens overlooking the town, climbing into large saloons to be driven to the most exclusive venues and homes, or to one of the many casinos, or down to the harbour to float on luxurious yachts. She even saw the former King Edward and Mrs Simpson from afar one time—but it was all just out of her reach.

The one place she could still live out her fantasy life was in the casinos of Monte Carlo and Nice. Attending most nights, she dressed to the nines, playing the part she'd seen in plenty of movies, but instead of impressing people with her posh voice and jewels, as she was used to doing, she had suddenly become a small, dull fish in a very big pond. Instead of being showered with invitations, all she really succeeded in was gambling away Mr Coradine's money.

After her third request for funds in a month, her grieving husband finally put his foot down and told her it was time to return home—but unbeknownst to him, she had no money at all. So Ethel set to work, only to become increasingly frustrated. Nice was full of wary wealthy people, vigilant French police and shop owners who found her usual ploys and stories unimpressive and transparent.

Ethel loved the Riviera, but without sufficient funds or means, the life she wanted most remained irritatingly out of reach.

She spun a tale to her hotel manager, truthfully explaining that she could not pay her account, convincing him that if she could make it back to England she could obtain funds from her doting husband and pay what was owed, plus a healthy bonus for his assistance. He lent her £40 so she could travel in the manner to which she was accustomed—then she promptly lost most of it in the casino. She stole away in the night with the one small suitcase she could carry, leaving behind a hatbox and two larger cases and their contents, along with a note for the manager explaining her goods were in lieu of her debt.

She slowly made her way back to England with the realisation that perhaps the French Riviera wasn't for her after all.

Instead of heading to her marital home, she returned to her old stomping ground, Blackpool. There she successfully passed various personal cheques, and swindled people out of accommodation and goods. Her faith was restored: a wealthy, well-spoken matron, she could still pull it off.

Ethel continued to cash cheques as she travelled around the country, until months later, in early July 1938, she was finally caught trying to pass one of her worthless cheques for ten pounds at a London garage.

———··———

Full of her own self-worth, Ethel was convinced she could wriggle out of the charge—it was for only £10, after all. What could she get from the magistrate? A slap on the wrist and a fine would be about it.

Ethel was surprised to find herself standing in front of a judge instead of a magistrate, but still felt confident to defend herself without a lawyer.

She stood in court and explained that she was the daughter of a distinguished Manchester citizen, and the wife of a retired Ceylon plantation owner and civil servant, and that it was all an unfortunate mistake—she thought the funds would be in the account.

The judge listened carefully and said it was indeed unfortunate that neither her husband nor father was in court to substantiate Ethel's claim, and ordered she serve three months in the second division at Westminster Gaol.

At least it was a little better than Strangeways. First division at Westminster was for murderers and political prisoners, it was probably the only time she was happy to be second class in anything.

Belatedly, Ethel realised she should have been in touch with her husband—perhaps that would have been the difference between a fine and gaol.

She'd get in touch with him again. But what to say to him? That she hadn't come back because she was still sick with grief?

Yes, that might work.

—————

Twenty years after first being banished to prison in England, she was back again. Depressed and isolated, she had plenty of time to contemplate what the future held. Ethel had not been in contact with her father for years; even though she had missed him, there was no way to easily explain her leaving her boys, and besides, Mr Coradine thought her father dead. She had now been officially married eight times, divorced three times, her eldest son would be 22 and she probably wouldn't recognise him if he walked past her in the street, her baby girl was dead, Frank and Basil would be fourteen and thirteen and were being looked after by the state as far as she was aware, and this was her third stint in gaol.

She once again decided she would try to lead a normal life. A happy, normal life.

Ethel came clean and wrote to Mr Coradine, laying all her appalling gambling stories on the table and apologising for not returning home. It was the gambling and the grief that kept her away from him, she pleaded—the gambling had caused all her current problems, and now she was in gaol. She hoped he would forgive her; she wanted to come home when she was released; wanted to stop gambling, and lead her life by his side.

William came to visit her in gaol. Over many tears, they shared past sorrows, fears, hopes and dreams for the future. William was horrified to find her in gaol because he'd stopped her funds; he promised he would make it up to her.

It was agreed that they should sell the Chelsea home and start up again somewhere new. Ethel explained to him gently that she needed to be busy, and asked if he would agree for her to start up a small business—a shop she suggested, in busy Blackpool. Though not having any knowledge of the area, William agreed, if it meant they'd be together.

They would look for a new home as soon as Ethel was released. A fresh new life beckoned.

———

Mr and Mrs Coradine bought a home, 217 High Cross Road, at Hardhorn Poulton, six miles inland from the Blackpool Promenade. It was a beautiful two-storey house, sitting on a prominent corner block with a large garden, and an easy train ride to Ethel's new business. William kept to himself in his retirement, while Ethel ran her artificial flower stall in the busy tourist district.

It was 1939, and war was all but imminent. Fresh flowers were almost impossible to buy, so artificial flowers, created from locally handmade felt, became popular. Ethel would purchase them cheap from local ladies and sell them on to tourists and businesses alike. She loved having her own business, engaging with people and selling her wares, and felt she did pretty well out of it.

World War II began. Once again Blackpool became a place where people went to try to forget, as well as being an aviation training ground for the Royal Air Force, bringing lots of recruits into the town on rest and recreation leave.

During the busiest summer months Ethel would sometimes stay in Blackpool, keeping her stall open into the twilight hours for those walking the promenade in the better weather. She took a room in a large boarding house at 2 Athlone Avenue belonging to an elderly woman, Margaretta Williams, happily exploring her old stomping ground, and catching up with her great love of movie theatres, leaving Mr Coradine at home.

In the summer of 1942 she met local businessman Thomas Livesey. Seven years older than Ethel, he described himself as a slate merchant, but it wasn't long until Ethel found out just how well off he was, and suggested they take in a movie.

Movies had changed so much from her youth; they all still had wonderful stories, though she preferred the romance and adventure films. The first of many movies they saw together was the Alfred Hitchcock thriller *Rebecca*, and they spent the evening talking about the movie, the stars of the film and the story itself.

From then on they met regularly, whenever Mr Livesey was in town.

William Coradine was not well, and Ethel didn't want to let this opportunity pass her by.

She had her next husband lined up.

21

MRS LIVESEY

Mr Livesey was indeed a slate merchant, but his wealth lay in money from his mother's side of the family. His maternal grandfather had left a job as a footman to work for a theatre manager in London as a young man, and a year later he was managing a theatre of his own in the West End. Within ten years he oversaw a theatrical empire and had made a fortune.

Prior to the Great War, Mr Livesey's grandfather owned and ran some of the best theatres on the West End, held two country manors and a racehorse stud in Ireland, before dying in 1915 at the age of 59. The male line of his family was cut to ribbons in the war, leaving Thomas' mother and an aunt, together with his business partner in the theatre, the main beneficiaries of over £50,000 (over $7.7 million). With the death of his mother and then father twenty years later, Thomas inherited a manor house in Surrey, together with his mother's remaining inheritance.

Thomas sold the manor house and bought five impressive investment properties around Liverpool, living off the rent, as well as the dividends from shares he purchased in a new product taking off around the world promising to outdo cotton: rayon. He was a man of means.

Ethel loved the fact that his money originally came from the theatre, and that the handsome movie star Roger Livesey was supposedly a distant relation, something that became a fact for her. Slowly but surely, she wheedled her way into Thomas Livesey's life.

Thomas was married, with children, and knew about Mr Coradine, whose health was steadily failing, and whom Ethel claimed she had never loved. She told him she stayed with her husband out of loyalty, and had a nurse look after him so she could carry on her social obligations.

After a few months Mr Livesey asked the charming Ethel Coradine to accompany him to the Isle of Man for a weekend away. Ethel readily agreed, and they headed off for their romantic getaway to the capital, Douglas, at the start of spring 1943. With distant family and business connections on the Isle, Thomas took the opportunity to mix business and pleasure on several successive weekends, more often than not with Ethel in tow.

They stayed at the fashionable Howstrake Hotel Majestic, owned by an enterprising middle-aged couple, Ellen and Leo Kane. Ethel and Mr Livesey always took separate rooms and pretended not to know each other during their stays, meeting in each other's rooms after dark. But they had to be careful, as Mrs Kane would regularly prowl the halls and lurk in bedroom corridors at night to make sure no hanky-panky was taking place in her establishment.

One afternoon Ethel was spending time in the hotel lobby while Mr Livesey was out visiting a business colleague. She was thinking about seeing a movie at the Regal when she spotted Mrs Kane, or Kanie as she was known to the locals, making her way towards her across the quiet lobby.

'Mrs Kane,' she said with a smile as Kanie came towards her. 'You have a lovely establishment here.'

'Thank you, Mrs Coradine, it is a little quiet at present, what with the war on and all,' Kanie replied.

'Indeed, will you join me? I was just thinking of having some tea, and I could do with some company.'

'Well, it wouldn't do any harm,' Kanie replied, looking around, and seeing her daughter called out, 'Evie, could you bring some tea for Mrs Coradine and myself?'

'Certainly mother,' her daughter replied, looking towards Mrs Coradine, who smiled in return.

Kanie sat primly across the table from Ethel. 'What brings you to the Isle of Man so regularly, Mrs Coradine?'

'Oh I need to get away for a while. It is so horrid in Blackpool presently, with all of this war talk—I truly think it is worse than the Great War,' Ethel replied. 'Not nearly as gay.'

Kanie looked a little startled, and Ethel realised her comment may have been unfeeling. 'Tell me a bit about yourself

Mrs Kane,' she said, changing the subject as she pulled out a cigarette.

'Not much to tell really, Mrs Coradine.'

'Nonsense,' countered Ethel, striking a match and efficiently lighting her cigarette. 'Are you a local, perchance?'

Kanie shook her head. 'No, I came here to work, before the Great War.'

'You must have been young,' Ethel remarked to the lady opposite, who gave a small smile at the compliment.

'Yes, I was, seventeen.'

'Did you come with your family, perhaps?'

'No, no, I was orphaned quite young. I trained as a waitress at the Imperial in Blackpool.'

'I know it well, a good hotel,' Ethel replied. 'How exciting for you though, at seventeen, setting off to a new country.'

Kanie gave a small smile at the memory. 'Yes, it was, but I worked hard and was kept busy.'

'Did you come here, to this hotel to work?' Ethel asked, looking thoughtfully at Mrs Kane as she drew on her cigarette.

'No, no, I worked at the Castle Mona at the start. That's where I met Leo, my husband—he was having a drink at the bar one night and spontaneously broke out into song.' Kanie looked across at Mrs Coradine, who sat relaxed, her cigarette dangling between her fingers, with the smoke slowly rising towards the high ceiling. Ethel gave her a smile and a slight nod, as if asking her to continue.

'When he finished singing, I told him he sung with such pathos,' Kanie said, 'and he told me it wasn't so much pathos as

Guinness! He did make me laugh.' She stopped talking as her daughter placed a tea tray on the table. 'Thank you Eva, I will pour.' Eva looked at Mrs Coradine, who gave a small smile and watched as the teenage girl walked away.

'Such a pretty daughter you have,' Ethel observed.

'Yes I suppose so, our Eva is a good girl,' Kanie mused absently, opening the teapot and peering in, then pouring the tea into the two china cups on the tray. 'Sugar? Milk, Mrs Coradine?'

'Both, thank you Mrs Kane—three sugars,' Ethel replied, watching as the efficient lady opposite carefully measured and placed the sugar into the cup, following with a dash of milk before handing it over.

'Thank you, that looks perfect,' purred Ethel. She picked the teaspoon off the saucer and thoughtfully stirred the sugar in. 'You said you have two hotels?'

'Yes,' said Kanie, settling back into her chair with her cup of tea. 'This one, the Howstrake Majestic, and the first Leo and I bought before the Great War, the Falcon Cliff.'

'You bought them? Your husband didn't own them before you were married?'

Mrs Kane gave a laugh, short and abrupt. 'Heavens no, we bought the Falcon Cliff first, and did quite well out of it after we rebuilt the old vertical railway car to bring guests from the promenade to the top of the cliff. We paid off that debt within four years,' she stated proudly, 'enough that we could buy this larger hotel before this war started, but we are finding it difficult to run two hotels with our son away fighting.'

'I, too, have sons away fighting,' Ethel said quietly, placing her cup and saucer carefully back on the table.

'So you know the worry,' Kanie replied.

'Indeed, Mrs Kane, I do,' confirmed Ethel. 'Both my sons are officers. Frank is in the navy, and Basil in the RAF—I do hope they will be alright.'

Mrs Kane nodded in understanding. 'Yes, I miss Douglas, and he is such a help with the hotels. I hope this war ends soon.' They both concentrated on the tea before them. 'Or we could sell the Falcon Cliff, it really is too much.'

Ethel looked at her. 'I may be able to help there,' she answered slowly. 'I know of several people who would be interested in purchasing a profitable hotel.'

'Really, Mrs Coradine?' asked Kanie hopefully.

'Yes, but I would like to have a look at it first.'

22

THE FALCON CLIFF HOTEL

Kanie drove Mrs Coradine to the Falcon Cliff that afternoon, explaining more about the hotel on the way. It had originally been built in 1836 for the Governor of the Isle of Man and had been converted into an impressive hotel in the 1870s. When Kanie and Leo bought it, it had been cheap as it was too steep for people to access easily, and was a fair distance by road from the tourist strip along the promenade, but Kanie could see the potential. Once they rebuilt the vertical railway, it became a tourist attraction in its own right, and locals and visitors flocked to the grand hotel.

As they drove through the large wrought-iron gates, Ethel learnt that the British Government was presently renting out the entire Falcon Cliff Hotel, and had been since the start of the war. The Isle of Man had multiple alien civilian intern-ment camps; Ethel had seen the fenced-off sections in the capital, where some 60 holiday houses and hotels were now full of internees, and had heard mention of other camps dotted around the island. Kanie explained there was a large male-only camp of nearly 1000 Finnish, German and Italian internees at Ramsey to the north; the whole of Port Erin to the south, and neighbouring Port St Mary was a camp for nearly 3000 women and children; and another camp for POWs and Fascists was established on the west of the island at Peel. Ethel had heard the stories of some of the inhabitants, and was now to learn that Falcon Cliff was the intern hospital. Thousands of internees now took the place of the summer tourists on the Isle of Man.

As Kanie went on at length about the beauty of the building, its high stone walls and castle-like turrets made an instant impression on Ethel, who was delighted by the thought of being mistress to such a large, imposing Gothic castle-like home. Falcon Cliff had once been *the* place to go, Kanie explained as they walked in, and would be again.

Ethel could see past the hospital beds lined up in the huge ballroom, and instead concentrated on the exquisite parquetry floors and leadlight windows facing inland, and the breathtaking views across the ocean on the other side. She pictured new modern furniture, servants and a life of luxury.

It was straight out of a movie set. She had to have it.

———•———

'How much does the army pay for Falcon Cliff?' Mr Livesey asked Kanie as they sat in her office at the Majestic.

Kanie looked at him carefully, and then to Mrs Coradine seated beside him. She was somewhat confused at the inclusion of another of her frequent visitors, Mr Livesey, in the meeting, and was starting to see a relationship between the two she was not entirely comfortable with.

'A reasonable stipend,' Kanie replied. 'Enough to cover your costs until this war ends.' She stiffened as Ethel reached over and placed her hand on Mr Livesey's leg.

'I love it,' Ethel said quietly. Mr Livesey smiled at her indulgently.

'You have seen the figures before the war started,' Kanie stated, drawing back the couple's attention. 'Run well, it will be a profitable hotel again.'

Mr Livesey nodded thoughtfully. 'Thank you, Mrs Kane, we would like to think about it.'

Kanie pulled herself upright and looked at the pair through her spectacles. 'I had not realised you were in business together,' she remarked.

Ethel smiled gently. 'We are to be married, Mrs Kane.'

'But you are already married, are you not?' she asked Mr Livesey. 'Both of you, to different people?' she added, looking between the two.

'Oh, no need to bother yourself Mrs Kane,' Ethel assured her. 'Mr Livesey here is seeking a divorce, and my husband is ill—he won't be with us much longer.'

Kanie looked momentarily in horror at them both. 'I thought your husband must have been serving, Mrs Coradine, I had no idea . . .' Her face closed and she looked blankly at the pair before her. 'I see. Well, Mr Livesey, I would appreciate an answer about Falcon Cliff promptly,' she said, raising herself from her chair. Mr Livesey and Ethel followed suit.

'Certainly Mrs Kane. I will speak with my lawyer and we will let you know,' he affirmed, grabbing his hat off the desk, missing the flash of anger that briefly spread over Mrs Kane's face.

Ethel saw it, and Mrs Kane held her eye.

'I run a respectable establishment here, and would appreciate it if you no longer frequented the Majestic on any of your future "visits",' she stated to Ethel.

Mr Livesey cleared his throat.

'Thank you Mrs Kane,' he stated. 'We will be in correspondence with you about your hotel.'

———•··•———

It was decided: they would move together to the Isle of Man.

Ethel formally closed up her stall and moved back to her home with the now totally bedridden Mr Coradine, while Mr Livesey formally asked his wife for a divorce.

Ethel dutifully stayed by William Coradine's bedside for his final weeks. On Friday, 15 October 1943, he passed peacefully away, leaving Ethel to be the dutiful widow. She promptly published a notice in *The Times*, visited the solicitor, put the house in Hardhorn Poulton on the market and waited for their purchase of Falcon Cliff to finalise.

On 26 November it was theirs. Ethel sold off the household contents of the Coradine home, withdrew all the money from her late husband's estate, packed up her prize possessions—namely her jewellery and clothes—and caught the plane to the Isle of Man. Mr Livesey greeted her at the aerodrome, then whisked her up to the clifftops and into their new home.

An army captain, Captain Harrison, headed the Falcon Cliff internee hospital. He oversaw the hospital doctor, who was himself an internee, and ran the hospital with the help of a storekeeper, clerk, three cooks, four sanitary staff, a stoker and four orderlies.

Ethel and Mr Livesey stayed in their room on the top floor, overlooking the large houses on top of the cliff behind them, until they could find a suitable alternative, and for the next few weeks Ethel had great fun lording around Falcon Cliff, charming the Captain and gaining all sorts of fascinating information—the local airfield had become a training ground for the RAF, bombing and air-to-air firing ranges had been set up, there was a ground-defence gunner's school and a top-secret radar installation, the army manned the intern camps, and the Merchant Navy regularly docked at the Isle, situated in the middle of the Irish Sea.

It was all exciting information, but war had never interested Ethel; she wanted to place herself at the top of Manx society, and she couldn't do that from a hospital, no matter how flash it was.

Then Captain Harrison gave her some information she found very interesting.

23

IVYDENE

Sitting behind Falcon Cliff were the more expensive areas of the capital. Some of the rich owners of the larger holiday homes dotted throughout the affluent suburbs had moved in permanently with the locals to escape the bombs falling on England. These, together with the upper members of Manx society, were who Ethel most dearly wanted to be seen with, but Falcon Cliff wasn't working out as a suitable home at all to entertain in, with all those sick internees scattered around the place.

So when Captain Harrison told her that the army was relinquishing a stately, fully furnished home in nearby Little Switzerland, currently being used to accommodate camp guards, she had to have a look.

Ivydene was everything Ethel could have dreamed of. Sitting high on the cliff overlooking Douglas Bay and the sea towards England, with a pillared entrance, the two-storey residence was made from local red sandstone, with stained-glass leaded windows and Tudor-style half-timber work of solid oak, topped off with a red tile roof. Inside was even more impressive, with carved oak panelling adorning the walls, and a magnificent oak staircase leading to the upper rooms. The garden too was breathtaking. The property was perfect to impress and entertain in, and Ethel easily convinced Mr Livesey that they should rent it. She promptly employed a cook, a butler and a maid and set about inviting what she called the 'cream of the Isle' to her home.

Even though they weren't married, she told everyone they were. Mr Livesey was negotiating a settlement package with his wife in exchange for the signed divorce papers, and then they'd fly back to a registry office in Liverpool to do the deed. In Ethel's eyes, they were all but married.

The new Mr and Mrs Livesey invited local professionals, businessmen, the rich and their wives to Ivydene, and Ethel's charm offensive went into overdrive. They held weekly bridge tournaments, extravagant dinner parties, garden parties and cocktail evenings as Ethel happily spent her and Mr Livesey's money.

Feeling settled and secure as the new Mrs Livesey, she felt confident enough to write once again to her father Frank, who for years had tried unsuccessfully to get in touch with his daughter and grandsons in Australia. The last he had heard from her was as Mrs Anderson living in South Australia with her two young sons, and then they had all simply disappeared. Ethel wrote a long letter from her new home at Ivydene, explaining how she had met and married William Coradine, moved back to England as his health deteriorated, and decided to leave the boys at Geelong Grammar School where they were settled for their final years of schooling (the last bit, of course, being untrue). She explained she hadn't had time to get in contact with her family since her return as she had nursed her husband through his debilitating illness. After his death, she met and married a Thomas Livesey, and was now living on the Isle of Man. She hoped her family was well and that they could see each other again soon.

The return letter was filled with a father's love and concern. He was delighted she was well and living so close, compared to Australia, and hoped his grandsons were doing well. He had sad news: her eldest son Frank Carter had been killed in the ongoing war, her mother had passed away just months before, and he was in the process of selling their family home. He was finding it hard to maintain their home as he grew older, but had misgivings about investing his money into another smaller house or investment property, and was contemplating moving in with her younger sister Mabel and husband Lionel.

The news of her son's and her mother's deaths did not overly sadden Ethel, but she did miss her father. Perhaps he would like to join them on the Isle of Man, she suggested—escape from Manchester for a while?

Mr Livesey was not overly impressed with the thought of his future father-in-law staying with them, so organised with Kanie for Mr Swindells to stay at their hotel.

Ethel's father arrived in March 1944 and moved in to the Howstrake Majestic, but when he had a mild stroke and became ill, Ethel insisted he be moved to Ivydene. Here she showed off her life to her father, who was impressed and pleased she was so happy and successful. Both she and Mr Livesey noticed that he had become a bit fuddled, and on Mr Livesey's advice Ethel suggested to her father that Mr Livesey become his power of attorney, and manage his affairs and all the paperwork involved with selling his home and two other properties in Manchester. Mr Swindells agreed and signed everything over to his new son-in-law.

The only cloud in Ethel's sunny sky was the fact that Thomas Livesey's wife refused to give him a divorce and was threatening to take him for everything he owned. Mr Livesey and Mrs Coradine flew back to Liverpool and met his solicitor to see what could be done. Soon afterwards, Mr Henry Gelling, legal advocate on the Isle of Man, was engaged to help Ethel change her surname by deed poll. As a recent widow and with the information she supplied, he found no impediments to this, and on 6 June 1944, her name was officially changed to Florence Elizabeth Ethel Livesey. This was the first stage in their plan to protect Mr Livesey's assets from his wife and children, and by the end of the month all of his assets—including five investment properties, £7500 (over $450,000) from his bank account, and his share portfolio— were transferred into Ethel's name to keep them away from his threatening wife.

Thomas continued his business affairs through Ethel's account, while the new Mrs Livesey set about developing a social circle among the rich and influential. She quickly spent up with the local storekeepers, refurbishing the already furnished Ivydene, and borrowing expensive glassware for her parties from the Kane family. She regularly flew to Liverpool and London to shop for the finest apparel, purchasing expensive jewellery from the Indian Diamond and Pearl Company, as well as the Liverpool jewellers Finnigans, and ordering the best food and wine she could obtain on the wartime black market for her parties. In less than six months she managed to spend more than £6000 (over $380,000).

At her many soirées, she revelled in telling her stories and nurturing new connections. She was especially delighted to meet one particular visitor to the island—a moviemaker from the Pinewood Studios. He lamented to Ethel the lack of funds in wartime England, and the fact that the British studios had been taken over by the War Office. With great excitement, a star-struck Ethel talked breathlessly with him about his latest film script idea, and at the end of the evening told him she had connections who she was certain would be able to arrange funding for the film.

In order to raise the funds, she and Mr Livesey agreed to sell one of her father's investment properties in Cheshire, 72 Groves Lane, at a bargain price to the tenant. But as soon as the money hit their account, Ethel started spending it. Of course, she couldn't help it!

Mr Livesey, meanwhile, was becoming disgruntled with their investment in Falcon Cliff—so it, too, was put back on the market.

With her father now settled into her home, Ethel felt that as a woman of social standing, she needed a charity to support.

She came across newspaper reports on the importance of the Merchant Navy to the war effort, and how the Merchant Navy Help Society was trying to raise funds to provide holiday accommodation and a clubroom in Douglas for its tireless workers and their families. They were aiming for £3200, but had only managed to scrape £100 together in the previous few years. Ethel had found her mission.

On Monday 31 July 1944, Ethel held a bridge drive with the local ladies for the Merchant Navy Help Society. She charmed all, including local Mona Douglas, who wrote for the Isle of Man *Weekly Times*. Mona was only a year younger than Ethel and was passionate about the island's ancient culture, particularly its music, dance and poetry, which Ethel pretended to take a great interest in, keen to make an impression.

'I find this country's culture truly unique,' Ethel enthused to the lady from the press, 'and I have of course travelled all over the globe, to just about every country.'

'Indeed, Mrs Livesey,' Miss Douglas replied. 'Where have you been?'

'The French Riviera of course, the Americas, New York is quite impressive,' Ethel replied airily, 'the remarkable Orient, Gibraltar, Northern Africa, so exotic,' she paused. 'New Zealand and the Pacific Islands, most of the Continent, and all around my home in Australia—other than the two poles I think I have been to most countries.'

'What was it that drew you and your husband to the Isle of Man?' the fascinated lady asked.

'Well Miss Douglas, I came over to see the island after spending most of the war in Liverpool and London, suffering through the horrors of the Blitz,' she began, 'and when we arrived I found that for scenery—even in miniature—it is the nearest approach to my homeland of Australia I have ever come across,' she pronounced, noting the appreciation spread across Miss Douglas' face. 'I find it enchantingly pretty, even in wartime, so my husband and I decided to take Ivydene,' she declared, sweeping her hand around to encompass her new home.

'And this charity event here today—do you have any particular interest in our Merchant Navy?' Miss Douglas asked.

'I feel that we all need to do our part for the war effort. I have two sons serving back in Australia, and coming to live on this island and seeing all the good that the Merchant Navy has undertaken throughout the war, I thought it a worthy effort to be involved in and support in any way I can.'

'And your sons?' Miss Douglas asked.

'Ah yes, my son Frank is a Lieutenant in the Royal Navy, and Basil is a Squadron-Leader in the RAF.'

'Indeed! You must be so proud of them both, Mrs Livesey.'

'Oh I am, Miss Douglas, but they are just doing their bit you know,' Ethel replied modestly. 'Now can I interest you in joining a four for bridge, perhaps?'

The afternoon was a great success, with many old Manx names among the crowd; games were played, with Frank Swindells drawing the donated raffle prizes. Mr Davies, the secretary of the National Sailors' and Firemen's Union, thanked them all at the end of the day, emotionally stating that despite times being economically tough, they had managed to raise over £63 (over $4000) towards the new club room, from one afternoon alone. To his knowledge it was the most money raised by a few ladies in a single afternoon. He turned and thanked Mrs Livesey extensively for her generosity in hosting the afternoon.

Those assembled applauded in delight, but none were beaming broader at Ivydene that afternoon than Mrs Ethel Livesey.

Over the next few months Ethel regularly flew to Liverpool and London, staying at Claridge's and the Adelphi, racking up large accounts, and shopping at the best establishments. The Adelphi was also the home of the American Red Cross, with Ethel making a point of entertaining the American and English officers, generously holding lavish parties there—her part in the war effort. It was during this time that she saw the damage in both cities from the Blitz bombings, and heard first-hand accounts from people caught in the fray. From all this, the Isle of Man was a welcome sanctuary.

Back at Ivydene she became actively involved with further fundraisers for the Merchant Navy. She organised speakers to visit Douglas to explain the critical role the Merchant Navy played in bringing vital supplies to the Isle of Man, and in all aspects of the war. It was a coup to host such important members of the Merchant Navy, and the locals were suitably impressed.

She insisted the balance sheet figures for the Ivydene events be printed in the press after each event, together with a letter from Mr Davies thanking her personally and explaining that Mrs Livesey provided all refreshments for her events, and had not deducted any expenses. She wanted all to know.

To the other fundraisers she couldn't attend, such as raffles, cigarette funds and bridge drives, she always donated—but never as generously as at her own events.

The businesses in Douglas were happy to give Mrs Livesey credit. Everyone treated her like royalty, and she was having a grand time. She racked up numerous accounts at the local grocer and wine merchant Victoria Stores, the butcher J.T. Brew, the confectionery and bakery Cain Brothers, R.C. Cain's dress shop, and A. Clucas & Co. for her daily order of fresh flowers to fill Ivydene.

Unfortunately for Ethel, her past was catching up with her. As well as owing money to the local business houses, she also owed her old Blackpool landlady Margaretta Williams a substantial amount, and had managed to avoid repaying it back, so far. But Mrs Williams had tracked down the elusive Mrs Coradine and she had been ordered to appear at the Blackpool registry of the King's Bench Division of the High Court. Ethel didn't want Thomas Livesey to know about this loaned money, he was under the mistaken impression that she had her own fortune.

Ethel waited impatiently for Thomas Livesey to sell off Falcon Cliff—she needed to keep in the good books of her new-found friends, many of them wives of tradesmen they owed money to. They had the hotel on the market but were not getting any bites from prospective buyers, so Mr Livesey decided to sell a property in England to tide them over.

Ethel watched as he sat at his desk in the office at Ivydene filling out the necessary paperwork. He looked up at her and pushed the paper towards her to sign, which she duly did. Rising from the desk, Mr Livesey said he would take it to the solicitor straight away, giving her a peck on the cheek as he departed. Her smile quickly vanished as she turned to look out across the garden to the sea, and to the English coast beyond. She heard the door close gently behind her as Mr Livesey left, and she turned back and sat down at the desk.

Ethel opened the draws and fingered through various forms, deeds, bank statements and her father's power of attorney, before placing them carefully back in order, closing the drawers slowly.

Contemplatively she looked down at the desk and ran her fingers slowly over the blotting paper.

———

By February 1945 Ethel's fantastic stories were beginning to unravel. It started one evening at Ivydene when her father was talking with her friend Mrs Cowin, sister-in-law to one of the local solicitors, and wife of one of the largest store owners in town.

'I'm sorry, Mr Swindells, Mrs Livesey was born in *England*?' Mrs Cowin asked as they sat in the lounge waiting for dinner to be served.

She looked across the crowded room and saw Mrs Livesey talking with her husband.

'Yes, Manchester,' Frank replied, taking a sip of his pre-dinner whiskey.

'Not Australia?' Mrs Cowin asked.

'Why no, she spent many years there, and her sons are of course still there—perhaps that is where you became confused,' he smiled.

'Perhaps . . .' Mrs Cowin replied, watching as Mrs Livesey casually placed her hand on Mr Cowin's arm.

Another occasion, this time a get-together at Mrs Cowin's two weeks later, proved more embarrassing for Ethel. Mrs Cowin had asked her accusingly just the previous day about being born in England, not Australia, and she thought she'd managed to laugh it off, blaming her father's failing mind. But Mrs Cowin didn't seem convinced.

To make matters worse, the movie producer from Pinewood Studios had returned to the island and was also at the Cowins that evening. He had been asking for the financial assistance Ethel had all but promised, and when he realised it wasn't forthcoming, and after he'd imbibed a few too many drinks, he decided to tell all in their social circle that night that he doubted Mrs Livesey could lie straight in bed! He stated loud enough for Ethel to hear that she was mentally ill and was suffering from delusions of grandeur, which was met with nervous laughter from those listening.

'She suffers the same malady as Adolf Hilter!' he declared.

Mrs Livesey stormed out without farewelling her hosts, leaving Mr Livesey to apologise and follow.

The next day, Ethel walked through the still icy March winds sweeping in off the Irish Sea as she made her way to the legal offices of Gelling and Cowin. She demanded to see Mr Gelling who had also been privy to her previous night's embarrassment, and was led into his rooms where she promptly announced that she wanted to sue the movie producer for defamation of character. Mr Gelling looked at her thoughtfully and gently advised Ethel that perhaps she should approach the man in question and advise him first of her intentions; surely this was a more civilised way of dealing with the situation?

Mr Gelling organised a private meeting between Ethel and the movie producer at Ivydene the following day. Gelling had explained the situation to him plainly before he had left the solicitors' office—with multiple witnesses to his defamatory comments towards Mrs Livesey, he could lose everything. Now sober and completely apologetic, he arrived at Ivydene. The pair spoke for some time alone in Mr Livesey's office, and after discussing what could be done to avoid a defamation case, Ethel saw him to the door.

As she walked back through the house she came across her father sitting in a chair with a rug over his legs. She told him she had a desire to see her boys again in Australia, but promised she would be back soon.

She made her way back into the office, pulled out the bank forms and starting filling them in, making her way through the list of properties owned by her father and Mr Livesey. Ethel already held Mr Livesey's property and cash in her name, and knew the funds were in her account from the recent sale of Mr Livesey's investment property, which she planned to take—but she also pocketed nearly all of her father's money, and put his properties on the market, leaving £539 in her personal Isle of Man account to cover her father's nursing and medical expenses.

She went to the airport and flew to London, leaving Mr Livesey with the last six months of creditors to contend with, and no ability to pay them.

———·—·———

In London, Ethel went to Australia House, home to Australia's High Commission—she needed to apply for a visa to travel back to Australia, and obtain a passport in the name of Livesey. Here she met the still apologetic Pinewood producer, who falsely stated he was a solicitor, and sponsored her application for a new passport and visa—but getting out of England wasn't as easy as it once was, as all shipping was now being given over to the war effort. There was one way, the helpful migration officer at Australia House explained: Ethel could apply for a visa on sympathetic grounds, but this could take some time. The producer stated to the officer that there was a genuine need for her to go to Australia and visit her serving sons; it was paramount. The deal he had struck with Mrs Livesey at Ivydene was that if he helped her get out of the country immediately, she would not sue. He wanted the possibility of a defamation case to disappear as quickly as the woman he was accompanying. He didn't care why she wanted to leave England, he just wanted her gone.

They left Australia House together, though quickly went separate ways. Ethel made it clear to the producer that he wasn't off the hook until she was out of the country. He in turn pulled strings with his War Office contacts to get her out of the country and out of his life.

Having taken all of Mr Livesey's funds, and most of her father's, Ethel decided to hide out while waiting for her visa to come through. So she rented a gentleman's estate in Wales, from Robert Gill, former high sheriff of the county and director of Lloyd's Bank. There she waited, at Brynderwen Hall, in a small country town, unsure what she would do if her visa didn't come through.

Two months later Germany signed an unconditional surrender, though the fight against the Japanese in the Pacific had not let up.

Ethel was fed up with the war. Wanting to find out how her visa was progressing, and whether the balance of funds from her property sales had come through into her account, she travelled back to London. The Welsh countryside, though beautiful in early spring, was boring!

Mrs Daphne Giblett—the photo presented in the 1923 divorce proceedings
of William Norman Giblett and Florence Elizabeth Ethel Carter nee
Swindells, who falsely called herself Daphne Vivienne Pollard at the time
of their marriage. The same photo confirmed to another husband, Midford
Stanley Hourn, that he too was a victim of bigamy.

WOMAN FACES FRAUD CHARGE

Man's Amazing Court Story

ALLEGED OFFER OF £5,000

AN amazing story of offers made to him by a woman customer of £1,000 and a shop in New Zealand, a guaranteed position in England with travelling expenses paid, and that she would settle £5,000 on him, was told in the Adelaide Police Court today by the manager of a drapery store at Henley Beach.

Florence Elizabeth Ethel Gardiner, aged 33, of Henley Beach, well-dressed brunette, with big brown eyes, was charged with having between October 26 and November 3, at Henley Beach, obtained from Coles & Hughes, drapers, goods to the value of £7 13/10 by means of false pretences that she was a station owner from New South Wales, and that her present husband was a member of the firm of Sargood, Gardiner, drapers, of Sydney.

PROMISED CHEQUE

Mr. J. P. Walsh prosecuted, and Mr. Gerald Rollison appeared for Gardiner.

Eric Francis Thompson, manager of Coles & Hughes, said that Mrs. Gardiner called at his shop on October 16 and said, "I am Mrs. Gardiner, from New South Wales. We are station owners. My husband has had a nervous breakdown, and we have taken a furnished house at 53 East terrace, Henley Beach."

She told him, said witness, that she would be wanting some drapery, and asked whether it would be convenient for her to open an account.

He replied, "We don't run many accounts ,but we make them out on the first of each month." She asked, "Do you do business with Sargood Gardiner, of first of each month. One asked, "Do you do business with Sargood, Gardiner, of Melbourne and Sydney?"

Witness said that he told her that he had done a little, Mrs. Gardiner then told him that her husband was one of the firm of Sargood, Gardiner. He took her to one of his assistants and said that it would be all right for her to supply Mrs. Gardiner with goods.

On November 1 Thompson said he received a letter from Mrs. Gardiner. He went to the South Australian Hotel at 11.30 a.m. next day. He had a long conversation with Mrs. Gardiner in the lounge. She said to him, "I expect you wonder why I wish to see you?" He

MRS. FLORENCE GARDINER snapped on her way to the court today.

Mrs Florence Gardiner trying to avoid the press on her way to court to answer the Coles & Hughes fraud charge—*The News* (Adelaide), Thursday 16 November 1933.

NEW SOUTH WALES

POLICE GAZETTE

AND WEEKLY RECORD OF CRIME.

No. 23.] WEDNESDAY, 6 JUNE. [1934.

NOTICE.

For Instructions as to Reports of Compilation of Police Gazette, vide No. 1 of this year.

[Extract from Government Gazette.]

APPOINTMENTS.

Chief Secretary's Department.

THE Governor-in-Council has approved of the following Police appointments:—

Acting Superintendent Albert Winter to be Superintendent 3rd Class,—from 1st May, 1934 (confirmation).

Acting Inspector Ernest Frederick Page Bower to be Inspector 3rd Class,—from 1st May, 1934 (confirmation).

FRANK A. CHAFFEY.

CRIME.

PERSONS WANTED.

Assault and Robbery.

Ashfield.—About 9.15 p.m. the 3rd inst., Violet Chandler, 126 Old Canterbury rd., Summer Hill, was assaulted and robbed of 1 green crocheted envelope-shaped handbag, about 9 in. x 4, containing a key; 1 pair of tortoiseshell rimmed spectacles in case, "Mark Foys" on case; and about the sum of 14s.; total value £2. Ident., except money. Whilst in that road by a man, NAME UNKNOWN

Sydney.—Vide P.G., 1934, pages 56 and 211. The above is a photograph of FLORENCE DUNKLEY, alias FLORENCE ELIZABETH GARDNER, alias LADY BETTY ANDERSON, alias PAMELIA PILKINGTON, etc., who is wanted on several charges of obtaining goods and money by means of false pretences (valueless

Falcon Cliff Hotel from the promenade, 1899.
The impressive entrance led to steep steps that
were later replaced with a vertical lift built by
the Kane family. It has since been refurbished
as an office building overlooking the bay.

'Ivydene', Little Switzerland, Isle of Man, the home Ethel rented with Mr
Livesey to live and entertain in throughout the later part of World War II.

NUFACTURING

ARRIED MAN'S GHT TO COURT

married man is quite within his rights in con-
ting matrimony with another girl when he is
his wife has walked out on him and will not
ack, the State Full Court decided today.

ief Justice (Sir Frederick
) laid it down that if a
ed he wanted a home and
did not have one because
had left him, he could
other girl, then ask the
rder his wife to return to
basis that if she did not,
iarry the other girl he had

before the court was an
Herbert George Harris, of
hose petition for a divorce
vife, Hazel Louise Harris,
St., Chatswood, on the
ier refusal to comply with
ler to return to him, was
by the Judge in Divorce
e Bonney) on the ground
cerity.
been stated in court that
contemplated marriage
er girl before bringing his
court, and the judge said
hink Harris really wanted
come back.
Court held that Mr.
ney was wrong, and that
entitled to his divorce,
ve him.

;E LOAN
BRITAIN

firror World Cables,
IGTON, Thursday. —
reports say that the
ates has agreed to
n £1,100 million.

says the loan agree-
e outcome of discussions
been going on for some
signed tomorrow.

U.S. Governments will
:ounce the loan figure
v in London and Wash-

Big Wedding Next Saturday

Mrs. Ethel Livesey, of Edgecliff, with Ting-a-Ling, her toy
Pekinese pup, given her as
wedding present by Dr. William
Cunningham. Mrs. Livesey is a
lover of Pekinese, and once
had a pet in England whose
sire was worth more than 3000
gns. Next Saturday Mrs. Livesey
will wed Mr. James Rex Beach,
of Woollahra.

Ethel Livesey with her Pekinese puppy Ting-a-ling in the garden of her flat in
Edgecliff, days before her highly publicised wedding to Rex Beech. *The Daily
Mirror*, 6 December 1945.

Big Wedding Postponed
BRIDE COLLAPSES;
RECEPTION GOES ON

PREPARED FOR
BIG WEDDING

Hotel Doors Closed To Rush

Mrs. Ethel Livesey, whose much-publicised wedding was due to take place last night, was reported to have collapsed at the last minute and, so far as is known, the wedding ceremony did not occur.

In the meantime, hundreds of guests assembled at a cocktail party reception at the Hotel Australia and scores of people waited outside Mrs. Livesey's home at Edgecliff to see her leave for the ceremony.

The guests nevertheless were still entertained at the Australia reception where an announcement was subsequently made.

It was not possible last night to ascertain whether the ceremony would be held at a later date.

Very wide interest had been taken in the plans for this wedding. Mrs. Livesey announced during the week that she would marry Mr. James Rex

Two of the bridesmaids arrive at Hotel Australia with the flowergirl Marigold Dezarnauld after the wedding was cancelled. *Truth* (Sydney), 10 December 1945.

Mrs Livesey sitting in the courtyard of her Edgecliff apartment days before her highly publicised society wedding. Despite the newspaper's claims, she is not wearing her imported Parisian bridal gown.

But There Was No Wedding

MRS. ETHEL LIVESEY with Mr. James Rex Beech, whom she was to have married in Sydney on Saturday night. The wedding, which was to have been the most elaborate for 10 years, did not take place (see story below).

POLICE WANT TO QUESTION

"HEIRESS"

Ethel and Rex Beech socialising prior to their planned wedding. *The News* (Adelaide) 10 December 1945.

Dressed For Wedding

MRS. ETHEL LIVESEY, Sydney's mysterious "cotton heiress", in the frock which she was to have worn at her wedding on Saturday. The wedding, however, was postponed at the last minute. Mrs. Livesey has left Sydney and is now believed to be in either Melbourne or Tasmania.

Still searching for the missing cotton heiress. This professional photograph of the bride was taken prior to the cancelled wedding. *The News* (Adelaide), 12 December 1945.

Below: Mrs. Ethel Livesey (right), the missing Sydney bride-to-have-been, whose disappearance has caused a national sensation. With her is her secretary, Miss Joy Dick. Mrs. Livesey is being sought in Queensland.

Still missing. This photo of Mrs Livesey and her secretary Joyce Dick at Edgecliff was published around the country as the police tried to track her down.

WEDDING RECEPTION WENT ON WITHOUT BRIDE OR GROOM

Ethel's elaborate wedding bouquet cost over four times the weekly wage at the time.

Although Mrs Ethel Livesey, who was to marry Mr James Beech in lavish style in Sydney, cancelled the wedding and disappeared, the 200 guests at the reception carried on the show. Above: The reception at the Hotel Australia at its height. Right: The four-tier wedding cake, which remained uncut.

This newspaper headline says it all.

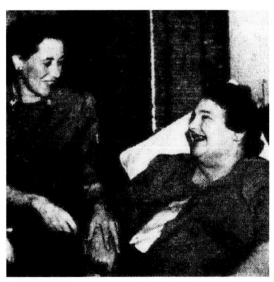

Mrs Livesey with one of her bridesmaids, Mrs Jack Sharpe, socialising before the upcoming society wedding of the decade.

Mrs Ethel Livesey, whose last-minute wedding cancellation in Sydney caused a society sensation, arriving at Sydney Central Police Court with her lawyer when she was charged with false pretences in South Australia. She was remanded to Adelaide.

Mrs Livesey leaves Central Court December 1945 with her lawyer Mr Lander after being charged with the 1933 case and is remanded to appear in Adelaide.

A relieved Mrs Livesey is granted
bail to appear the following day in
the Central Court.

Bride missing, gifts returned, the
mystery of the wealthy cotton
heiress keeps the world enthralled.

Mrs. Livesey Mystery Grows

LADY VANISHES, GIFTS GO BACK

Just who, or what, and more particularly
just now, WHERE is Mrs. Ethel Livesey, the
buxom bride-to-be, who, last week, intrigued
Sydney and, in fact, Australia, by collapsing
almost on the steps of the matrimonial altar?

*Mrs. Livesey disappeared last Sunday morning
after her much-publicised wedding, with its
attendant resplendent reception at the Hotel
Australia, had been cancelled. All efforts to trace
her since have failed, although it is believed she is
still in N.S.W. and probably still close to the city.*

Last traces of the prepara-
tions for the projected wedding
with Mr. Rex Beech, Sub-
Treasury official, have vanished, too. Scores of valuable
wedding presents, showered on
Mrs. Livesey by the friends
and acquaintances she had
made in all walks of life in
Sydney since she burst into
the social whirl here, have been
parcelled up and many re-
turned to the senders.

MRS. ETHEL LIVESEY leaving the plane after her arrival at Parafield from Sydney last night.

Mrs. Livesey Expects "Fair Deal" in S.A.

Mrs Livesey arrives back in Adelaide belatedly by plane after being delayed in Melbourne and being questioned over an outstanding fraud case from 1936.

'Was Miscarriage Of Justice,' Says Freed Mrs Livesey

ADELAIDE, Saturday.—Relaxing in the quite sanctuary of her son's home at Flinders Park—with a glass of whisky and soda in her hand and her stockinged feet on a hassock—Mrs. Ethel May Livesey, central figure in the Sydney glamor wedding which did not come off—to-day told a "Truth" reporter of her thoughts and feelings since her conviction by an Adelaide criminal court jury on two 13-year-old false pretence charges.

Mr. Justice Mayo had released Mrs. Livesey on bond following her conviction by an Adelaide Criminal Court Jury on two charges of obtaining goods from Adelaide firms by false pretences in 1933.

MRS. LIVESEY said to "Truth": "Somehow I have survived a terrible ordeal. My conviction was a gross miscarriage of justice and I have suffered much. However, the past is behind me and I look to the future with confidence.

"I cannot speak too highly of my three legal advisers, nor can I over-emphasise the moral stimulant provided by those nearest and dearest to me, added to which the kind thoughts and gestures of the public generally have sustained me."

"Since my conviction I have received more than 300 letters of sympathy, many offers of homes and numerous gifts of flowers—all of which I appreciate immensely. Now I am going home to Sydney and, I hope, to peace."

About that wedding: I spent £250 on the reception and that did not include the drinks. Then, almost everyone forsook me because of something they had heard about me. Well, I am writing a book of my life. My story will rock Australia—I can promise you that, and it gets better as the years go by.

"Since my case began, I have received more than £800 letters and telegrams from all over Australia and New Zealand.

Mrs. Livesey says she is not 19 stone, but 14 stone. Her Sydney address will be Gowrie Oals.

Mrs. Ethel Livesey, says she will write a book.

After being found guilty on a now thirteen-year-old charge, Mrs Livesey gives another interview to her favourite paper from the yellow press, *Truth*.

Crowd Throngs Central To See Mrs. Livesey

ESCORTED BY HER SOLICITOR, MR. W. LANDER, Mrs Livesey leaves Central Court.

A grim faced Mrs Livesey and her lawyer leave the Adelaide Central Court during her 1946 trial.

'Was Miscarriage Of Justice,'
Says Freed Mrs Livesey

ADELAIDE, Saturday.—Relaxing in the quite sanctuary of her son's home at Flinders Park—with a glass of whisky and soda in her hand and her stockinged feet on a hassock—Mrs. Ethel May Livesey, central figure in the Sydney glamor wedding which did not come off—to-day told a "Truth" reporter of her thoughts and feelings since her conviction by an Adelaide criminal court jury on two 13-year-old false pretence charges.

Mr. Justice Mayo had released Mrs. Livesey on bond following her conviction by an Adelaide Criminal Court jury on two charges of obtaining goods from Adelaide firms by false pretences in 1933.

MRS. LIVESEY said to "Truth": "Somehow I have survived a terrible ordeal. My conviction was a gross miscarriage of justice and I have suffered much. However, the past is behind me and I look to the future with confidence.

"I cannot speak too highly of my three legal advisers, nor can I overemphasise the moral stimulant provided by those nearest and dearest to me, added to which the kind thoughts and gestures of the public generally have sustained me."

"Since my conviction I have received more than 100 letters of sympathy, many offers of homes and numerous gifts of flowers—all of which I appreciate immensely. Now I am going home to Sydney and, I hope, to peace."

About that wedding: I spent £250 on the reception and that did not include the drinks. Then, almost everyone forsook me because of something they had heard about me. Well, I am writing a book of my life. My story will rock Australia—I can promise you that, and it gets better as the years go by.

"Since my case began, I have received more than 4000 letters and telegrams from all over Australia and New Zealand.

Mrs. Livesey says she is not 19 stone, but 14 stone. Her Sydney address will be Gowrie Gate.

Mrs. Ethel Livesey, says she will write a book.

Mrs Nan Glover (alias Mrs Ethel Livesey) is charged with more counts of false pretences in Tasmania in 1949.

Mrs. Livesey sent to gaol

Buxom Florence Elisabeth Ethel Livesey (52) was sentenced to two months' gaol at Adelaide Court this week for having stolen four pieces of crystalware valued at £4 17s 6d and a pair of boots worth 10s 6d from the home of the man who employed her as a domestic four years ago.

Mrs. Livesey clasped the dock rail and broke down sobbing when she pleaded guilty to the charges.

Since she arrived from England as a bride at 16, Mrs. Livesey has hit the headlines fairly often, the most notable occasion being when she was to be one of the principals in a lavish wedding in Sydney, which did not come off.

Mr. C. J. Philcox (for Mrs. Livesey), in a plea for leniency, in court this week, said that his client had a most unhappy background.

Mrs. Livesey

Ethel's past catches up with her. She is charged and gaoled in Adelaide in 1950 for larceny of goods dating back to when she was on the run in 1946.

24

FORTUNE TAKEN TO AUSTRALIA

With her new passport in hand, stamped with the hard-to-come-by visa, Ethel Livesey stole back to Liverpool and paid £165 ($10,000) for a first-class berth on the Swedish merchant ship *Barranduna*.

The brand-new ship was heading to Port Pirie in South Australia to collect a load of lead—the first commercial ship to make the journey since the outbreak of World War II. Unusually for a cargo ship, the *Barranduna* had first-class accommodation for twelve people. All the berths were full, and as Ethel walked into her cabin, she exclaimed in delight: it was filled with 40 large bouquets of fresh flowers. The eleven other passengers remarked on them in wonder—fresh flowers in wartime!

Little did they realise she had ordered them all for herself.

The *Barranduna* left Liverpool on the morning of 3 July 1945, with Ethel playing the well-to-do lady visiting her serving sons back in Australia, though she found the passengers more subdued than she would have liked.

Most of the other passengers were taking the rare opportunity to travel back to their homeland, now that the Germans had surrendered the European front of the war. Mr and Mrs Barr Smith and their 23-year-old son were heading back home after arriving in England on business with their family's company Elder Smith & Co, and were returning to Australia with Mr Barr Smith's sister Christine McGregor. Mr and Mrs Hall, another late-middle-aged couple, had similarly been stranded in England through the war. The remaining passengers were all middle-aged men—company directors, a solicitor, a plastics manufacturer and a wool buyer, and not much fun at all as far as Ethel was concerned. They were all anxious to get home rather than kick their heels up, and none seemed overly interested in Mrs Livesey's stories. Despite her wealth, the trip was turning out to be rather dull.

A little over a month into the trip, the mood changed. The passengers were stunned in awe and disbelief when the Captain gave them what scant details he had of the American atomic bombings in Japan, at a place called Hiroshima.

With the Captain's next message, a week and a half later, a sense of relief swept through the ship: the Japanese had surrendered. The war was over.

When the ship docked in South Australia on 27 September, Ethel decided to try and track down the two sons she had abandoned twelve years before.

Nineteen-year-old Basil was living in Flinders Park in Adelaide, with a woman nine years his senior, Sylvia Schutze, who was the daughter of his foster parents, and who had a six-year-old daughter from a previous marriage. Basil welcomed Ethel back into his life, but at nineteen and without a job, he was struggling. With an abundance of funds—£40,000 worth, she boasted (about $2.5 million in today's money)—Ethel took pity on him and set about negotiating the purchase of a newsagency for Basil to run.

Frank, however, proved impossible to find; it would later turn out that he was living on the open road, working on stations in the outback, taking jobs wherever he could.

Ethel herself was soon on the move again, to live life as she had always wanted, without a thought for the future.

———·•·———

Ethel was the heaviest woman the booking clerk had ever seen when she was booking her flight from Adelaide to Sydney via Melbourne. Knowing that weight meant a lot on a plane, he insisted Mrs Livesey get on the scales, and even he was surprised to see she weighed in at 275 pounds—just short of twenty stone, or 125 kilograms. Ethel insisted that the scales were faulty.

Arriving in Sydney in the first week of October, Ethel went straight to the posh eastern suburbs on the harbour, where she felt quite at home with her new wealth, and rented a classy ground-floor apartment in Edgecliff. She even hired a private secretary, Joyce Dick, who helped Ethel find a suitably reputable doctor who could see her promptly for her female health problems.

Dr William Cunningham was head of gynaecology at Sydney's King George V maternity hospital, and came from a respectable eastern suburbs family. Ethel told him all about her wealthy family back in England, and how she had returned to Australia to visit her two sons, who had served in the armed forces and were both rapidly promoted and serving with distinction. Dr Cunningham was so taken with Ethel that he asked her to join him and his wife Ella at their next dinner party, where she was introduced to Flight Lieutenant Jack Sharpe and his wife.

When she found out that Jack was born in Wales, Ethel exclaimed in joy. She told them all of her wonderful home, Brynderwen Hall, in Bwlch-y-Cibau. Jack knew of the great estate in Montgomeryshire, and had also heard of the Swin-dells cotton family, and together with the huge amounts she was spending, Ethel had all the collaboration she needed: Mrs Ethel Livesey was indeed a cotton heiress, from a good family, with considerable wealth.

That evening she also met and befriended Lizette Brunning-hausen, whose wealthy widowed mother, Mary Dezarnauld, held large family dinners every Sunday night for her five adult children and their families at her home in exclusive Bellevue Hill. The affable Mrs Livesey was popular with all of the family and their friends, and was subsequently asked to the best houses.

Through Mrs Dezarnauld she was introduced to Lady Mable French, and Ethel went out of her way to cultivate their relationship. She became a regular visitor to Lady French's four-storey mansion in Sydney's Macquarie Street, overlooking the Botanic Gardens. The building had once housed her first husband Sir Herbert Maitland's surgical rooms, but since his death twenty years previous had become his widow's residence.

Lady French had met her second husband, Sir Frederick French, in 1939, when he managed to bring a passenger liner full of passengers through the German submarine lines to Australia, the last passenger ship to safely make it through from England. Sir Frederick was promoted to Commodore and, though safe in Australia, felt he had to go back and do his bit for the war, so he steered the passenger ship back to England, without incident. He finally returned to Australia in 1944, when he officially retired, and Sir Frederick and the widowed Lady Maitland held a quiet wedding in Vaucluse, advising their grown-up children, who were all overseas, after the event.

Ethel and Lady French became confidantes, sharing the experiences of their lives with each other. They had both married young and lost their husbands, Ethel telling Lady French that her husband *James* Livesey was killed in a bomb raid in London, where she had been working as an air-raid warden. Mrs French's two sons were overseas, one working and settled in England, the other in India working as a doctor; Ethel's two sons were decorated officers in the air force and navy, serving in Australia during the war, so far away from her in war-torn England. And Lady French, too, had lost a child. They had so much in common.

Lady French's late husband had also left her an impressive holiday home, Lethington, at Pittwater on Sydney's northern beaches, which Ethel came to love as much as the good lady— even though it was a bit too far away from the city for her liking—and sought to be included in the Palm Beach set.

Ethel happily recollected her own stories to Lady French of her château in the French Riviera, her manor house in Wales, and her cliff-side home on the Isle of Man. She told great stories to Lady French and her friends, of entertaining the Duke of Windsor and his friends on her yacht in the Riviera, and of her enormous wealth as the daughter of a successful cotton millionaire linked to the Coats cotton empire, and intimated that she personally held large holdings in Courtaulds, the rayon manufacturer, and that by her voting strength alone was able to control the destiny of the company. (She forgot to mention, of course, that the shares, a much smaller amount than she claimed, had actually been Thomas Liveseys.) With some modesty she also shared with her friends that she endowed hospitals and clinics, helped repatriate wounded servicemen— and despite spending large sums on her charitable pursuits, was left with an embarrassing amount of wealth, which she could spend as she pleased.

Ethel's tales became ever larger than life at each subsequent event she attended. She was to host and be seen at dinner parties, garden parties, bridge nights and charity balls, where she happily made large donations to all of her friends' charities and repeated her fantastic stories of great wealth with flair.

Ethel was in the society to which she felt she truly belonged, she had money to burn, and she was on a roll.

25

MR BEECH & THE WEDDING
OF THE CENTURY

Just a month after arriving in Sydney, Ethel was introduced to a middle-aged civil servant by the name of Rex Beech.

A divorcé, James Rex Beech had originally come to Australia in 1912, hoping to seek his fortune as a miner. He had then fought in the Great War, married and divorced in short succession, and was now working for the Federal Treasury in Sydney. He was from a fairly well-off family back in England, and like Ethel spoke with a clipped British accent.

Mr Beech and Mrs Livesey were often seen together over the next month. When it was decided they would marry, her new friends were happy for the wealthy widow.

With all her new money, Ethel decided to have a wedding that would be talked about for years to come. She certainly succeeded.

Her engagement to Rex Beech was celebrated in style with an elaborate party at the Australia Hotel for her closest group of society friends, where she spent over £300 (nearly $20,000) in one evening, gleefully showing off to all her platinum engagement ring, set with 43 aquamarines and diamonds.

Her wedding ring was being especially designed and contained another 32 diamonds, costing over £150. She also had an extravagant wedding dress made by Edward Molyneux, designer to the stars and creator of royal wedding gowns, and was having it flown in from his studio in Paris. Cattleya orchids in shades of mauve, purple and cyclamen were being specially grown in a hothouse outside Sydney for her bridal bouquet, which was to cost £50 alone, as well as bouquets for her four bridesmaids; the church and the reception were also to be filled with extra large and expensive floral arrangements. Doves were to be released from the magnificent sandstone All Saints Church in Woollahra as the bride and groom emerged, and the wedding service itself would feature a full choral ceremony, with Australian soprano Miss Jean Hatton and world-renowned Australian flautist Neville Amadio performing. The Australia Hotel was booked for the reception, with an unlimited supply of the best French champagne; an enormous four-tiered wedding cake topped with another elaborate floral arrangement was to be the centrepiece of an extravagant buffet, the likes of which had not been seen since well before the war.

The tabloids got a decent whiff of the wedding, which was being touted as *the* society wedding of the year, and ran exclusive stories about the twenty-stone bride to be.

Ten days before the December wedding, Ethel was sitting in the garden of her Edgecliff flat with her secretary Miss Dick in tow, speaking with a young guest reporter with the *Daily Mirror*, who was a society lady herself brought in by the editor to find out more about the wedding and its bride. The editor thought her perfect to interview the wealthy cotton heiress everyone was talking about. The accompanying photographer snapped photos of Mrs Livesey and her secretary, in the court-yard of her Art Deco flat, and had to supress a smile as the large lady before him tried to hold her new toy Pekinese puppy.

'This is Ting-a-ling,' Ethel explained as she held the squirming puppy up to her face for the photographer. 'Dr Cunningham gave him to me as a wedding gift,' she added, letting the relieved pup drop to the ground and run over to Miss Dick.

'An unusual gift,' the lady reporter noted, watching the pup jump against the secretary's leg.

'Not at all. He knew I used to own this wonderful breed back in England before the war,' Ethel replied, straightening her clothing. 'I was once offered 3000 guineas for my best stud dog, but refused of course.'

'Of course,' the reporter remarked, trying not to appear disbelieving, scribbling Ethel's comments into her notepad. 'I'm sure our readers would love to know more about yourself, Mrs Livesey. You were born in Britain, I understand?'

'Indeed, Manchester—my father runs a large cotton empire, stretching from Manchester to London. And my mother is a cousin to the Coats cotton family—you may know of them?' she asked. The reporter nodded as Ethel continued, 'I am the eldest of two daughters, so will inherit the business.'

'Have you been in Australia long?'

'Only a few months,' Ethel replied. 'I came out as I have some business interests that needed attending, and my two sons Frank and Basil Livesey from my previous marriage have been out here serving in the Royal Navy.' Once again changing her story slightly.

'They will be coming to the wedding?'

'Of course,' Ethel replied.

'Of course,' the reporter repeated, looking at her notes. 'And your fiancé?'

'Yes, Rex, he is the son of Mr James Beech of Whitby House in Staffordshire and is an officer in the Treasury,' she said. 'He served in the AIF and was at the Anzac landing.'

Lady Elizabeth again nodded as Ethel continued, 'We plan to have our honeymoon at the Carrington Hotel in the Blue Mountains. Mr Beech and I expect to return to England in March, by way of Monte Carlo, where I have a château,' she added. 'I also have homes on the Isle of Man, and a home, Brynderwen Hall, in Wales.'

The reporter looked up at her curiously. 'Indeed,' she remarked. 'And your wedding, Mrs Livesey—who will be in the bridal party?'

'My dear friends,' she replied, 'Mrs Cunningham, wife of the well-known surgeon Dr William Cunningham, will be my matron of honour, and I have three other wonderful attendants as well—Mrs Jack Sharpe from Woollahra,' she said, purposely mentioning the exclusive Sydney suburb, 'Mrs Sweet, also from Woollahra, and Miss Dick here from Elizabeth Bay,' she added, smiling over to her secretary. 'And I cannot forget the lovely Marigold Dezarnauld, who will be our little flower girl.'

'How old is Marigold?' Lady Elizabeth asked.

'She would be seven,' Ethel replied absently, before continuing. 'Sir Frederick French, former Commodore of P&O liners, will be giving me away—his dear wife Lady French suggested it—and Mr Beech will be attended by his good friend Mr Leslie Booth, Dr Cunningham, and Flight Lieutenant Jack Sharpe, RAAF.'

'And I understand you have booked the Australia Hotel for 500 guests, yet you've been in the country only a few months, is that right?'

Ethel smiled at her incredulous tone. 'Why, yes—we originally intended to ask only six close friends, but I have made so many friends since I arrived that the numbers of guests kept growing. I had to ask my hairdresser and some of the delightful local shop girls and sales managers I have come to know, and of course the cream of Sydney society,' she added smugly.

'It sounds like quite a wedding, Mrs Livesey.'

'Indeed, it will be,' Ethel replied.

Mr Beech was not impressed at the articles appearing in the press about his upcoming wedding.

'It will be fine, Rex, no need to worry,' soothed Ethel, straightening his tie and flicking some imagined dust off his new jacket.

'If you say so, Ethel, but I do wish you hadn't said I'd been at the Anzac landing—it simply isn't true!'

'Really? I thought you had been, silly me. Now let's not worry about the gutter press, let's enjoy our evening.'

Rex Beech nodded, turned and held out his arm for Ethel to loop her arm through as they walked towards the impressive entrance door to their friends' house for a social evening playing cards.

Ethel had first met Mac McDonald, a successful lawyer and ex-politician, at one of Mrs Dezarnauld's Sunday dinners, as he was married to one of her daughters, May. Mac opened the door and greeted the charming Ethel Livesey and her fiancé Rex Beech.

'Ready for the big day?' he asked.

'As ready as I'll ever be Mac,' she replied. 'Only five days to go, but I do wish the press weren't so terrible—neither of us can get much peace.'

'I am sure they will let up eventually,' Mac said reassuringly. 'Your wedding has caused quite a bit of excitement, but do come in—I think May has put us on a table together.'

They entered to find card tables set up in the drawing room and most of the other guests already there, and it wasn't long before they sat down to play. The first games went well for Ethel on Mac McDonald's table, and on the last she won yet again, with an incredible hand. Mac sat back as everyone rose for some refreshments, trying to remember the cards that had been dealt; it left him feeling uneasy.

When his wife suggested they swap tables, Mac positioned himself so he could watch Mrs Livesey. His surveillance was keen enough to spot Mrs Livesey reaching for a handkerchief in her bag; he remembered her doing something similar in their games as well. He felt *sure* she was cheating—but why would a woman of her standing sink so low? It didn't make sense.

Later that evening, after farewelling their guests, Mac decided some discreet enquiries might be in order.

More newspapers had taken up the story of the wealthy heiress's marriage the following weekend, and the extravagances planned.

'Oh, listen to this one!' began Ethel, reading from the newspaper in front of her. 'Mrs Livesey speaks with a gentle cultivated voice, and her two-handed generosity and democratic outlook have made her a popular figure . . . that is lovely, isn't it?' looking up at her doctor as he tried to take her pulse, and then to her secretary.

Joyce nodded absently. She'd had about enough of newspaper reporters. They were constantly harassing her on the telephone, or lurking outside the building, always wanting more details, and as Mrs Livesey's address had been printed in one of the papers, there were even people lining up outside the flat on Edgecliff Road to catch a glimpse of the large middle-aged bride to be.

Sitting in a lounge chair with her puffed-up feet on a cushion, the room filled with fresh pink gladioli, Ethel looked up at Dr Cunningham as he warned her, 'You need to rest, Ethel—your blood pressure is too high for my liking.'

'Thank you Bill, I will be fine,' Ethel replied with a gentle smile as her secretary handed her a cup of tea and some papers without a word.

'I don't know what to think, Joyce,' she said to her secretary as she scanned the pile of letters and notes handed to her along-side her tea. 'So many!'

'Over thirty requests yesterday alone,' Joyce replied wearily. 'All wanting charity of some sort.'

'Yes, but there are also these wonderful letters from people—everyday people wishing me luck . . . '

'If you don't mind me saying, Ethel,' Dr Cunningham inter-jected as he started to pack his medical bag, 'you have been far too generous.'

Ethel let out a big sigh and was about to reply when the tele-phone rang with a loud shrill, making Joyce jump. The rattled secretary took a breath and quickly picked up the receiver. 'Hello,' she said.

Ethel watched as Joyce frowned at the person on the other end. 'No, she is not available—all of this unwelcome publicity has made her quite ill.' Ethel and Dr Cunningham watched as the normally placid girl fired up. 'It has been the exaggerated reports in *your* paper that has caused all of these problems!' Halted by an interruption, she continued, 'Your reports on the amount of money being spent are likely to cause problems with the Federal Prices Commissioner for Mrs Livesey if they continue.' Joyce sat looking at Ethel as the reporter quizzed her further. 'Yes we are getting sick of it, we all are,' she said, looking away. 'The matrons of honour and groomsmen are being constantly pestered, and the groom is also upset by the publicity!' She stopped and again listened. 'No, she has nothing to say. Good day to you,' and hung up.

She looked over at Ethel, who was taking a sip from her tea. 'I will be glad when this wedding is over,' Joyce said.

'I understand completely dear,' Ethel replied, placing her cup back onto its saucer, as the phone rang again.

Joyce snatched it up in annoyance. 'Hello!' she said savagely. 'Oh, hello Reverend. Yes, yes, she is here, but can't come to the phone I'm afraid . . . I see, yes, yes, I will inform Mrs Livesey. Thank you Reverend. Yes, see you soon.' She placed the receiver down carefully and looked over towards her boss.

'That was Reverend McCook—he is coming over and would like to talk to you about moving the wedding.'

By the time the Reverend arrived, Joyce had managed to get Rex to the flat. Mrs Livesey was nearly in tears, Rex sitting stiffly beside her chair, patting her arm in condolence as Dr Cunningham again checked her blood pressure.

'Oh Reverend!' Ethel exclaimed, as the man who was to marry them walked into the room. 'I am sorry I am unable to stand to greet you—my ankles have swollen drastically and I, I . . .' she tried to continue, bursting into tears.

The Reverend stood in the middle of the lounge room, his hat in his hands in front of him. 'Please don't apologise Mrs Livesey, this is a trial for all of us.'

Rex stood and extended his hand, which the Reverend gratefully shook. 'Thank you for coming, Reverend. Now, I understand you want the wedding ceremony moved?' he asked, as Ethel tried to stifle a sob behind him.

The Reverend nodded in agreement. 'Yes, I am sorry to do this, but there has been unprecedented interest in your wedding from so many—the press in particular. I am more than happy to perform the ceremony, but am deeply concerned something may happen to the church or surrounds.'

'Do not trouble yourself, Reverend. We have spoken with Dr Cunningham here, and he is happy to have a smaller ceremony at his home,' Rex said, Dr Cunningham giving a small nod of approval.

Fighting back tears, Ethel hiccupped, 'What about the doves ... the flower arrangements ... the guests ... the, the choir?' she managed to get out between sobs. Noting her fiancé's glare, she swallowed and took a deep breath. 'It is not that I wish to appear ungrateful, Reverend, but surely it is too late to cancel all of these arrangements?'

'As I said, I am more than happy to perform the ceremony, Mrs Livesey, but I must insist that it be moved.'

Rex walked over to Ethel and squatted uncomfortably down beside her. 'We will still be married Ethel, the wedding itself is not cancelled, and with a few telephone calls we will be able to set this right.'

She returned his tight smile and again hiccupped. 'What of the reception?' she asked quietly. 'We can't cancel that—the food, the ice sculptures, 500 people ...'

Rex stood and let out a sigh. 'No, we will go ahead with the reception.'

'Good,' she said, wiping the tears from her eyes and trying to sit up straight. 'It would be a shame for everyone not to see my dress.'

——— · ———

The wedding, now to be held in Dr Cunningham's Darling Point home, was to take place at 7.15 p.m., with limousines conveying the bridal party to the much-anticipated reception at the Australia Hotel.

The bride, her four bridesmaids and little flowergirl Marigold were dressed and having photographs taken at Mrs Livesey's flat, when there was a knock at the door. Marigold's mother went to answer it and was surprised to find the bridegroom standing there, with Mac McDonald.

'We would like a word, Mrs Livesey,' Mac stated, walking into the lounge room, followed closely by Rex Beech.

The photographer snapped another shot of the bride as Mrs Livesey saw her visitors standing in the doorway. 'Mac! Rex! What are you doing here? Surely it is bad luck for the groom to see the bride before the wedding!' she joked, and then stopped at the two grim faces of the gentlemen in front of her.

'We would like a quiet word, Mrs Livesey,' Mac stated again.

Ethel was taken aback by his tone, but quickly pulled herself together in front of the others. 'Certainly, Mac, but can it not wait? It is rather an important day.'

'No Mrs Livesey, it cannot,' Mac replied. 'We need to speak, in private.'

'Right then,' Ethel said, disengaging herself from the group, looking around the crowded flat. 'Perhaps the bedroom would be more private,' she added, stumbling as she went to move off. Rex, standing close by, made no effort to help. It was Ethel's secretary who went to her aid, and steadied her.

'Would you like me to accompany you, Ethel?' Joyce asked gently.

'If you don't mind dear, I do feel a little woozy,' she said before turning to the other ladies in the room. 'We won't be a moment, I'm sure.' With Joyce's help she walked down the short hallway to her bedroom, the men following close behind.

Mac closed the door behind them and Ethel looked at him quizzically. 'What on earth is this about, Mac? What could possibly be this urgent?'

'Your name is Florence Elizabeth Ethel Livesey, is it not?' he asked.

'Yes,' she replied, looking from Mac to Rex in apparent confusion.

'You changed your name by *deed poll* in June last year, not by marriage,' he stated.

'Oh, I can explain that,' Ethel laughed. 'Mr Livesey's wife wouldn't give him a divorce.'

'You were living with a married man?' Rex asked angrily, speaking for the first time.

Ethel pulled back her shoulders. 'Yes, but he didn't love his wife.'

'I thought you a moral woman,' Rex said quietly.

'I *am*, Rex!' Ethel replied. She took a step towards him, but swayed and half collapsed on the bed, her secretary rushing to her side, helping her sit on the end of the bed, as she looked up at Mac and Rex uncertainly.

'Your maiden name was Florence Elizabeth Ethel Swindells?' Mac stated calmly.

'Yes,' Ethel said a little uneasily, not so sure where Mac was going with his line of enquiry.

'You were married to a Mr Anderson?' he asked.

'Yes,' she said quietly, 'but he was already married . . . ' Registering the shock on her secretary's face, Ethel blurted, 'I didn't *know* when I married him, Joyce!', turning to Rex in exasperation.

'Your sons are not Frank and George Livesey as you told us. They have the name Anderson,' Rex stated. 'What else have you lied about?'

'Nothing, Rex, *please*—I was *ashamed*, I had unwittingly married a bigamist!' she implored.

'Then why did you not seek a divorce?' he demanded.

Ethel had no reply.

'We also found an outstanding warrant on fraud charges for you, Mrs Anderson,' Mac stated. 'From 1933, in South Australia. Do you deny Florence Elizabeth Ethel Gardiner, alias Anderson, is you?'

'Where did you . . . ?' She began, then stopped herself and looked imploringly at Rex, and then Mac.

Ethel's shoulders slumped and she seemed to sink into the bed. 'That *was* me, but I was young and had been deserted by my supposed husband, and it was the Depression,' she started. 'I had two young boys to feed, you must understand. I am not proud of that time, but I had to get back to England and seek help from my father.'

She saw Rex soften ever so slightly, and reached her hand up towards him, pleadingly. 'Please, Rex, you *must* understand.'

'Rex, on this information I must strongly suggest that you not marry this woman,' Mac declared. 'And I also suggest we leave,' he added, steering Mr Beech towards the bedroom door.

'Rex!' Ethel squawked, 'Rex, please, the wedding . . .'

'Come on Rex,' Mac ordered, pushing him through the door. Ethel turned to Joyce.

'He will be back,' she said quietly.

Joyce laid Ethel down on her bed sobbing; still dressed in her bridal gown, Ethel was inconsolable. Joyce told her to rest as she made her way out into the lounge room, where the confused bridal party looked at her expectantly.

'The limousines are here!' Mrs Sweet, one of the bridal party, relayed excitedly. 'They're just putting the white ribbons on them—there is *such* a crowd down there, there must be a hundred people in the square.'

'The wedding is off,' Joyce announced. All the ladies stared at her open-mouthed, before Mrs Sharpe finally asked what they all wanted to know. 'But why?'

'I am not certain,' Joyce began, looking at the other members of the bridal party staring at her so intently. 'But I don't think there will be a wedding today.'

They gasped at each other in confusion as the photographer and his assistant quietly packed up and slipped out the door. 'What should we do?' asked Mrs Cunningham. 'We will never get through that crowd.'

'I suggest you go down and take two of the limousines,' Joyce said, taking charge. 'Go home, the crowd will be waiting to see Mrs Livesey.'

She turned to Mrs Cunningham. 'I need to telephone your husband and tell him Mrs Livesey has collapsed.' Quickly adding as concern crossed over the women's faces, 'She is alright—just a little shocked I think. Perhaps, Mrs Cunningham, you would like to wait here for him,' she suggested as Mrs Cunningham nodded her head.

As the ladies collected their belongings and farewelled each other uncertainly, Joyce picked up the phone. While she waited for the operator to pick up the call, she glanced over at the large dining table, overflowing with wedding presents, and couldn't help but wonder if the bride and groom would ever open them.

———

Outside the Australia Hotel, a crowd had gathered, hoping to catch a glimpse of the wealthy bride everyone was talking about. Hundreds lined Castlereagh Street from 7 p.m. on that warm, early-summer evening.

At 7.15 p.m. hotel staff rolled out the hotel's famous red carpet, and by 7.30 p.m. the crowd had grown to enormous proportions, watching guest after guest file past in their finery—ball gowns that hadn't seen the light of day since before the war, new gowns for those who could afford them, dinner suits, and many returned servicemen in dress uniform. The numbers waiting outside continued to swell as invitations were checked and guests were admitted.

The guest reporter from the *Daily Mirror* was waiting to enter the reception with some of her old Sydney University friends. Some in her party had been responsible for a university prank several years previously, in which English visitor Sir Evelyn Wrench was 'kidnapped' and dropped off at the Sydney Crematorium in the dead of night, after refusing to give a lecture to the handful of students who had bothered to turn up. He had then refused to attend the vice-chancellor's luncheon organised after his lecture, embarrassing both the vice-chancellor and the university. The students were not charged, but had to write a letter of apology; no matter, they had embarrassed the smug Pom. Now they were graduated doctors and engineers, and some had recently returned from armed service, and the opportunity to have some fun at the expense of the 'cotton heiress' proved too tempting. Outside the Australia Hotel they held telegrams inviting them to the reception, supposedly from the bridegroom, addressed to the likes of Sir Mompas Slayme, Mr Humphrey Bender, Prince George Toobetooa of Fiji, Lady Bolingbroke, Miss Catherine Aragon and Lady Belladonna Schnitzel.

The crowd oohed and aahed at each new arrival, speculating on who they were—then reports filtered through that gatecrashers were trying to get in. A few in the crowd decided to also give it a go, but were quickly turfed out, to the amusement of their companions.

Two of the bridesmaids and the flower girl arrived. The excitement in the crowd was electric as they waited for the bride.

Fifteen minutes later the red carpet was rolled back up, and there were rumours that the doors to the banquet room had been barred.

The crowd became restless. Many began to chant 'Where is the Bride?' to the tune of 'Here Comes the Bride', and a police inspector and five constables were needed to control their mostly good-natured irritation.

Inside the hotel, in the vestibule outside the first-floor banquet hall, the guests waited, with loud murmurings passing between them, wondering what was going on. Why were the doors barred? Should they go or stay? Where were the bride and groom?

Shortly after 8 p.m., the doors to the banquet room opened and the guests were finally allowed in. The *Daily Mirror* reporter would later write that many openly gasped at the splendour of the feast before them, and the variety of expensive liquors on offer, all lit by candlelight and gas lamps because of the electricity restrictions still in place after the war. Chefs carved and waiters fluttered around with drinks. The orchestra tuned their instruments for the 'Wedding March', but by 8.30 p.m., broke into another song.

At 8.45 p.m. Mr Baydon Johnson, the banquet manager, mounted the orchestra dais and addressed the guests.

'Ladies and gentlemen,' he began. 'I have been asked to announce that the hostess will not be able to be with us.' He stopped as gasps from the guests turned into speculative murmurings. 'She would like,' he said loudly, trying to get above the hubbub, 'she would like you to carry on, as if she were here. Enjoy yourselves.'

As he descended from the dais, the buzz among the guests in the dimly lit room became louder and louder.

———·—·———

Joyce took a cup of tea in to Mrs Livesey, who was lying on the bed as if stunned, still dressed in her Molyneux gown.

'Mrs Livesey?' she said quietly. 'Ethel?'

Ethel turned to her and it seemed to take a moment for her to focus on her secretary standing before her with the proffered cup of tea.

'Oh Joyce,' she said. 'Thank you, but I will get up,' clambering to the edge of the bed and rising unsteadily.

'Careful,' Joyce urged, placing the cup beside the bed and helping her stand.

'The pills Dr Cunningham gave me seem to have left me feeling a bit hollow,' Ethel said with a crooked smile. 'What time is it dear?'

'Past nine.'

'I understand,' Ethel sighed, sitting back down onto the bed. 'I know the wedding is off now.'

Ethel reached for her tea, which Joyce brought towards her. Holding it with shaking hands, Ethel looked back up to Joyce: 'I need to speak with Rex. Could you see if you can get him for me?'

———·—·———

Ethel waited in vain all night for Rex to arrive.

Finally, in the early hours of the morning, Joyce fell into an exhausted sleep on the couch while Mrs Livesey, still in her wedding dress, paced beside the windows, smoking furiously and looking out whenever she heard a car pass.

She had to admit, it was over.

At 4 a.m. Ethel went into her room and reluctantly changed out of her wedding dress.

She started to worry about how much Mac did in fact know. She hadn't thought back to those events in 1933 for a long time, but if the warrant was still valid, she knew she could be arrested.

She dragged the telephone into her room and quietly made a call.

After coming back from the Australia Hotel, the *Daily Mirror* guest reporter had spent the night making notes. She and her friends had shared a hilarious night, watching as the minions had descended on the extravagant banquet and free champagne like a plague of locusts, especially once it was known the mysterious bride was not coming.

She had a chat with one of the bridesmaids and gleaned some details of what had occurred in Mrs Livesey's flat earlier that afternoon, and was amused when the little flowergirl in her pink dress and silver slippers had crawled under the table and fallen sound asleep.

She sat thinking about the woman she had interviewed, and her supposed family back in England. She'd ask her newspaper editor about interviewing someone in England for their comment on the extraordinary woman. She felt sure there was much more to Mrs Livesey than anyone had suspected.

———·—·———

On Monday morning Mac went to the local police station. All through the previous days, he and the others in the wedding party had been harassed by reporters. No, they hadn't heard from Mrs Livesey, and frankly didn't want to.

Later that Monday morning, two police officers arrived at Number 1 Cumberland Court to see the caretaker removing Mrs Livesey's nameplate from the list of tenants at the entrance to the building. They made their way up the stairs, into the foyer, and knocked on her door.

'Who is it?' asked an uncertain female voice on the other side.

'Police,' they replied.

Joyce opened the door warily. 'How can I help you?' she asked.

'We would like to speak to a Mrs Ethel Livesey,' explained one officer to the young woman before them.

Joyce sighed and opened the door wider. 'You'd better come in then.'

The police walked in and stood looking around the lounge area as Joyce slowly closed the door.

'She is not here I'm afraid.'

'And you are?'

'Oh sorry, I'm her private secretary,' she said. 'Or was.'

'I see,' the officer said, bringing out a notepad. 'And do you know where Mrs Livesey is now? We would like to talk with her.'

Joyce shook her head. 'No, I am sorry, I don't know exactly—but she did leave me a note.' Making her way to the desk, she rifled through some papers, pulled out a small note written on cream bond paper, and handed it to the police. 'I'm just sorting through all of this paperwork, but I'm not sure where to send it, or what to do,' she reflected uncertainly. 'She says she is going to Melbourne,' she added as they read the note.

'Did she take anything with her?' one of them asked.

'Some suitcases, hatboxes, and a few of the letters from wellwishers, as far as I can see,' Joyce replied, looking at the overflowing pile of wedding presents on the dining-room table. 'I guess I had best return those,' she added quietly.

'And what do you know of Mrs Livesey?' asked one of the officers.

'What I *thought* I knew seems to be untrue . . . I thought I knew *everything*, but it appears I didn't—nobody does.'

———•———

Ethel had hired a private car to pick her up in Edgecliff before daybreak on the Sunday morning. She had the driver take her to the railway station at Moss Vale, 90 miles south of Sydney, where she told him she would connect with the Sydney–Melbourne train.

The driver duly dropped her at the station, then helped unload her bags, six suitcases and two hatboxes, into the reception area.

Ethel paid him handsomely in cash, thanked him, and re-iterated that she would be pleased to see Melbourne again.

Once he had driven away, she purchased a ticket back to Sydney.

26

POLICE WANT TO QUESTION HEIRESS

At Sydney's Criminal Investigation Branch (CIB), a warrant arrived from South Australia for Mrs Florence Elizabeth Ethel Livesey, alias Gardiner, alias Anderson, alias Stevens, alias Lockwood, alias Pamela Pilkington, alias Gloria Grey. The warrant was for the twelve-year-old charge of fraud for the outstanding Coles & Hughes drapery case in Adelaide.

The case was handed to Detective Constable Lance March and Constable Bill Bushby. DC March was soon inundated with information from Australia and overseas, and had also received a request to speak with Mrs Livesey from Adelaide detectives about the outstanding fraud charge, as well as another from a solicitor acting for Mr Livesey wishing to speak with her when she was found. It appeared that her wealth had been obtained through Mr Livesey, who apparently had not been her husband, but a scandalous de facto partner instead.

Mrs Livesey wasn't an heiress—that much had been established by some simple enquiries to her family back in Britain—and there were rumours of her being seen all over Australia.

All of this information was doing DC March's head in. He needed to talk with the woman, and it was his job to find her.

'We've had reports of her in Tasmania, Melbourne, Sydney and even Brisbane,' Constable Bushby said to his boss in exasperation, 'and it's been less than a week!'

DC March was going through the papers on his desk. 'The Brisbane sighting?' he asked, without looking up.

'Well, that was a bit of a red herring,' the constable replied. 'Mrs Livesey was booked on a train to north Queensland, leaving Brisbane two days ago, but when our colleagues up north went to the station, she wasn't on the train.'

'And what of that sighting in Sydney?' asked DC March.

Constable Bushby shuffled through his papers and pulled out the one he was looking for. 'An acquaintance of Mrs Livesey states he saw her walking down George Street on Thursday,' he read. 'But she wouldn't be that brazen, would she?'

'Everything I've read so far about this woman makes me think she could be,' replied DC March. 'The fact is we just don't know, but she would be hard to miss.'

'Yeah, but the Vics were fooled, weren't they?' the constable replied. 'They thought they had her at that swish St Kilda hotel, booked in under a false name, but it turned out to be another fat woman, using her own name! I wouldn't want to be there when they explained why they thought she was Mrs Livesey.'

Constable Bushby held up one of the newspapers towards his boss. 'Did you see this one? This article reckons people should look out for her around butcher shops! Being that large, she'd have to eat a *lot* of meat!' he laughed, but stopped when he saw his boss's expression.

'Yes, quite,' DC March replied, looking at the vast array of newspapers piled in front of them, all filled with stories and speculation. 'There is plenty of press coverage and interest,' he said slowly, thoughtfully tapping the papers in front of him. 'So let's use them—let's see if we can flush out Mrs Livesey, wherever she is hiding. My bet is she is still here somewhere.'

———·•·———

Back in England, Ethel's sister Mabel was surprised to see a reporter standing at her door. He was from the *Daily Telegraph* and had a few questions about her sister.

'I frankly don't know how many times my sister has been married,' she told him on her doorstep. 'It may be four or five times, or even more. I know she's had the names of Coradine, Anderson and Livesey. I believe there may have been others.'

When asked where Ethel had lived in England, she replied, 'She had a house on the Isle of Man, which I understand was rented. She is a jolly woman, fond of getting about, but I know little about her private affairs.'

———·•·———

A reporter from London's *Daily Mirror* travelled to the Isle of Man and found Mrs Livesey's father sitting in his room at the Howstrake Hotel Majestic, a rug over his knees, reading a shilling novel.

'I don't know what all this fuss concerning my daughter is about,' Frank Swindells stated as the reporter sat opposite him. 'First the police, and now you. Whatever it is, you can talk to her in Australia. I don't wish to say anything.'

The reporter handed him a copy of the *Truth* newspaper from Australia and watched as the old man slowly and carefully read the two full pages about the supposed cotton heiress and the wedding that didn't happen. When he'd finished, he placed it down on his lap and looked over at the young man.

'Before she left,' he began, 'she told me she was returning shortly, but now I read this.'

The reporter left the old man staring out the window, refusing to say anything further. Gently closing the door behind him, the reporter went off to question anyone he could find on the Isle about the amazing Mrs Livesey.

And he was thorough. As well as interviewing locals, he made enquiries about the Swindells family in Manchester. They were indeed into cotton in a big way, and were one of the largest and wealthiest manufacturing families in Lancashire—and even had big trade in Australia—but a family representative wanted it known that Mrs Livesey was not related to them. On returning to London, the reporter went to Australia House and interviewed the customs official who had processed Mrs Livesey's application to travel to Australia just months before.

'In her interview, she told me she had gone to Australia with her husband in 1919,' the official stated, 'and after his death she had married again in New Zealand in 1935, then returned to England, leaving two boys at Geelong Grammar School. She also stated that one of the boys joined the navy and the other enlisted in the RAAF, and that her second husband had died in 1943. She then told me that she desperately wanted to return to Australia to see her boys, and was given a visa on sympathetic grounds.'

All wonderful fuel for the fire.

27

SOCIETY WOMAN ARRESTED!

DC March's appeal through the newspapers seemed to have paid off, with an anonymous tip that Mrs Ethel Livesey was hiding out in a boarding house in the western Sydney suburb of Chester Hill, fifteen miles from the city. It was the weekend, early Sunday morning, 23 December—two weeks since Mrs Livesey had left her Edgecliff flat.

Driving the big black CIB car, Constable Bushby pulled up outside the ramshackle house at 19 Jocelyn Street. Both of the officers looked through the dawn light towards the front door.

'Doesn't look like a place a rich dame would stay in,' the constable observed.

'It might, if she's on the run,' replied DC March.

'Just hope it's not another wild goose chase,' Constable Bushby said. 'Those other three leads were duds—I think we've found every Jolly Nelly in Sydney so far,' he remarked, referring to the local sideshow 'fat lady' people paid to see.

'We have to look into them all,' DC March replied, reaching for the car door handle. 'Come on, let's go.' As he stepped out of the car, he heard Bushby muttering about working all the time and it being almost Christmas.

DC March knocked on the door and a light in the front room came on. 'Hello?' he called out.

The door opened and, to their surprise, standing in front of them dressed in an enormous silk nightdress and heavily embroidered silk dressing gown was Mrs Livesey, the woman they had been chasing for the last two weeks seemingly without a break. She stood in the dawn light blinking blearily at them.

'Mrs Ethel Livesey, my name is Detective Constable March, and this,' he said, indicating his still slightly stunned colleague, 'is Constable Bushby. We have a warrant for your arrest.'

The buxom woman nodded her head, as if she'd been expecting them.

'We need you to accompany us to the Criminal Investigation Branch.'

'I will need to get dressed,' was her only reply, as she turned back into the house, the two officers following.

'Where are the other members of the household?' DC March asked her. 'The landlady, are they sleeping?'

'Mrs O'Hagan and the others were out at a party last night, I don't think any of them returned,' replied Ethel, as she turned into what must have been her room. 'Excuse me gentlemen, I need to dress.' And gently closed the door.

'Bill, go outside and wait near her window in case she tries to do a runner.'

The constable nodded and turned to go. 'That would be a sight to see—don't think she'd fit out the window!' he mumbled.

DC March paced up and down the hallway, pulled out his watch and looked at the time. How long does it take to get ready?

'Mrs Livesey!' he called through the door in loud exasperation. 'Mrs Livesey, we *do* need to get to the station.'

'I won't be a moment Inspector,' she called back sweetly. 'I just need to make myself presentable.'

'It is Detective, Mrs Livesey, not Inspector,' he corrected her, as the door opened and her bulk filled the doorway.

'Sorry Detective,' she said. 'I tried to be as quick as I could.'

He looked her up and down; her robust figure was now enclosed in a neat blue and black frock, a well-cut edge-to-edge black jacket, her hair coiffured into place with a black pillbox hat sitting at a rakish angle on top. In one hand she held her clutch bag, the other a smart leather briefcase.

'I will need to talk with my lawyer,' she stated.

DC March looked at her steadily. 'You'll be able to make a call from the station. I need to tell you that the arrest warrant is for . . .'

'I know, Detective, it's been in all the papers,' Ethel replied.

———·••·———

Ethel had already employed the best lawyers money could buy. She had been in George Street, as had been reported to the police, to meet the banquet manager of the Australia Hotel, Baydon Johnson and his wife Ruby, to thank them for their help in preparing the wedding reception, and to apologise for the mess that had been left after Rex Beech called it all off. They had both been so supportive, and she told them she was glad to consider them true friends.

She tried to contact several of her other society friends, and finally managed to talk with Lady French over the telephone, only to be told that no one wanted to associate with her. When Ethel hung up the phone, she had burst into tears of anger and frustration, turning to Mrs O'Hagan, the owner of the boarding house she was staying in. If only she could tell her society friends the truth—*her* truth—everything would be all right again. Mrs O'Hagan suggested she visit a solicitor she had heard was quite good, a Mr William Lander.

Ethel disguised herself as best she could and again made her way into the city, to 79 Elizabeth Street, down the road from one of her favourite shopping haunts, David Jones. After hearing her version of events, Lander quickly got in touch with a barrister friend, Mr Simon Isaacs, and they worked out what she should do.

It had been Ethel herself who rang and anonymously told the police where to find her. Sick of being on the run, she wanted to clear the air, tell her side of the story, get her life back. Her lawyers had assured her that if she faced up to the charges she'd more than likely get off the minor fraud charge, and she was now ready.

Pulling up outside the CIB headquarters after her arrest, Constable Bushby found to his annoyance that the press had been tipped off. Groups of reporters and photographers had gathered, but were unable to get a decent photograph or interview Mrs Livesey as DC March and Constable Bushby whisked her rather unceremoniously into the building.

Mr Lander arrived not long after and sat in on the interview. All day was spent at CIB headquarters, and after several interviews Mrs Livesey was released on bail, into Mr Lander's care, until a court appearance the following day. Lander drove his client to his office in the city, where they met a male reporter from the local *Truth* newspaper.

As they sat in oversized armchairs in the reception area outside Mr Lander's deserted office, Mr Lander served them, and himself, a stiff Scotch.

'Thank you for seeing me Mrs Livesey,' the reporter began. 'I understand you would like to tell your side of the story?'

Ethel took a sip of her Scotch and nodded. 'Indeed, I have been far too trusting,' she said. 'Everyone has been telling me so.' She paused and took a deep breath, 'I *do* need to tell my side of the story.'

'Well thank you,' the reporter replied, opening his writing pad. 'The arrest must have come as a shock, did it not?' he asked.

'Oh yes, it was indeed, I don't know how I endured the ordeal of the early morning surprise arrest, and the long day imprisoned in that cell, until dear Mr Lander here managed to get me out,' she said smiling briefly at her solicitor, before turning back to the reporter. 'It took forever, as you can imagine, to organise the formalities of securing the £200 bail on a Sunday, but it would have been so much worse if it hadn't been for the kindness of the police matron.

'That woman,' she continued, leaning forward, 'has seen so much trouble in her time that she is one of the most understanding persons I have ever met in my life . . .'

The reporter tried to steer Ethel back to her own story. 'We understand that you have been in Melbourne and Goulburn since you left the morning after the day arranged for your wedding?' he enquired diplomatically.

'I, as a free British subject, am entitled to travel wherever I care!' Ethel declared. Mr Lander cleared his throat, and Ethel softened her tone. 'I know a lot of people may feel inclined to give me a trial in their own minds, and in their own hearts. But I will say this about myself, that I am a woman who has had a heartbreaking experience, and that if I deserve nothing else, I at least deserve sympathy.'

'How has your experience been heartbreaking, Mrs Livesey?' the reporter asked, curious.

'Well,' Ethel replied, sitting back into her chair, 'I have had a lot of adverse and humiliating publicity. Reporters and photographers have dogged me, and harassed me. I have been followed and worried. Every friend I've met seems to have been questioned and closely cross-examined about me, and so much suspicion and innuendoes cast. I have been almost frantic with distress. People I thought were my friends, and whom I had lavishly entertained, deserted me in my hour of need.'

'But some believe that you courted publicity?' the reporter remarked, thinking back to the articles before the wedding.

'That is not correct. I am a very generous woman and I like to entertain my friends. Because of my hospitality, I attracted the attention of some sections of the press, which seemed to hang around the fringe of Sydney society,' she stated, with barely hidden disdain. 'I never encouraged anyone to photograph me or to discuss my life or become interested in my relaxation.'

'Do you feel some bitterness, then, Mrs Livesey?'

'Until tonight, I did feel hurt and bitter,' she replied. 'I felt that some people wanted to hurt me more than I have already been hurt in my life. I felt that some people wanted to pry into my private life. Surely that is unfair and unjust!' she railed. 'But, we are approaching the season of goodwill, so I wish to extend it even unto those who may feel unfriendly to me.'

'I see,' said the reporter as he finished jotting down his shorthand, then looked up at Mrs Livesey carefully. 'You have had a varied life, then, Mrs Livesey?'

'Yes, I have travelled the world, and I have had many vicissitudes. But though I have not hurt a man or woman in my life, I have been the butt of some people who seem to get cruel satisfaction by pointing the finger of scorn at anyone, no matter who they may be,' she huffed, her blue eyes flashing in anger. She took a deep breath. 'The only person I have ever hurt is myself, that is because—womanlike—I have been too trusting and generous.'

She picked up her glass and looked straight at the reporter. 'I have not the slightest doubt that I will be able to establish my entire innocence of the twelve-year-old charge in Adelaide, and that I will be clearly vindicated. But on the advice of my lawyers I prefer not to say anything on this subject.'

She paused, then suddenly declaimed: 'Perhaps I could add this. I would like to appeal to my hundreds of good friends out there, to withhold judgment until everything has been straightened out—then they may judge me, with an unbiased mind.'

The reporter nodded and tried another question. 'Have you any plans for Christmas, Mrs Livesey?'

'No, how *can* I?' Ethel retorted, then let out a long sigh. 'Your question recalls, with a pang, that Christmas is with us, and that I am under a cloud.' She paused a moment, looking earnestly at the reporter. 'That cloud will soon pass away. All I ask is that I be allowed to lead my own life and that everyone will encourage me with some silent sympathy and that a fair proportion of the community will say, let the poor woman have an Australian "fair go" before passing any judgment on her . . . I would like to wish through your paper a Merry Christmas to everyone who can be kind enough to feel this way!'

———••———

Christmas Eve saw Ethel arrive at the Central Police Court in style. Thanks to the *Truth* article, curious crowds had gathered along Central Lane, spilling out both ends onto George and Pitt streets in the hope of seeing Mrs Ethel Livesey, with the police having to clear the road several times before she pulled up in a big green sedan.

She looked a million dollars, wearing her expensive brown dress embroidered with dainty blue flowers; a smart lightweight black coat; black kid gloves, with matching bag, hat and short veil; her only jewellery two rings, and large pearl earrings and necklace. At first she appeared upset by the number of cameras flashing around her when she alighted from the car.

One woman in the crowd outside the police court entrance called for three cheers for Mrs Livesey from the crowd. 'Come and show Mrs Livesey that there is a side of society other than those who dropped her like a hot coal!' she called out, starting up the cheers.

Mrs Livesey seemed delighted and managed to smile and wave to the crowd, shouting out, 'My stepsons fought for you!' to another cheer, as her solicitor and barrister led her into court.

Ethel was charged as Florence Elizabeth Ethel Gardiner before Mr Duncan Parker SM (Stipendiary Magistrate, equivalent of a District Court judge today), who suggested she could sit behind her counsel. Her barrister Mr Isaacs glanced at the packed courtroom and replied, 'I think she would prefer to stay in front of the dock, where she is more or less hidden from the public gaze.'

Mr Parker looked at Ethel and nodded serenely, and with all eyes following her she made her way behind the wooden screen at one side of the court that shielded her from the view of the public gallery.

Detective March was brought before the court and testified that Mrs Livesey had admitted in custody that she was the woman charged, and that she had failed to appear at the Adelaide Quarter Sessions in December 1933 to answer the charge.

They then brought in Detective Constable Clement McGrath, who had travelled up from Adelaide with the original 1934 warrant issued after Ethel didn't appear in court to answer the fraud charge on the third day of the case the previous December. DC McGrath told the court that he had issued the warrant to Mrs Gardiner in the hall outside the courtroom at 9.50 that very morning, and that she had admitted being the person named. 'She told me,' DC McGrath started, pulling out his notepad and reading from it, '"If I am granted bail I will give you my assurance, I will appear. It was not my fault I absconded before." I therefore ask the court that Mrs Gardiner be remanded into my custody to be taken to South Australia, to be further dealt with according to the laws of South Australia.'

Mr Isaacs stood to question the Adelaide detective. 'When did you leave Adelaide, Detective?' he asked.

'Monday night,' DC McGrath replied.

'And before you left, did you make enquiries as to when this charge would be heard?'

'I did,' he replied. 'It could be listed in the January sittings for Monday 14 January.'

'I see,' Mr Isaacs seemed to contemplate, 'three weeks away. And tell me, Detective, in a twelve-year-old case, are all of the witnesses available?'

DC McGrath hesitated a little before replying. 'I do not think all are available,' he admitted.

'Have some left South Australia?' Ethel's counsel asked.

'We think so,' replied DC McGrath, 'and another may have died.'

Mr Isaacs turned to address Mr Parker. 'The fact that Mrs Florence Elizabeth Ethel Gardiner and Mrs Livesey are one and the same person will not be contested, and in fact is readily admitted by my client,' he stated, looking towards Ethel, who looked back at him steadily. 'My client has not the slightest doubt that she will be able to establish her innocence on this twelve-year-old charge,' he attested, turning back to the court. 'She has not been evading arrest, but has merely been living in quiet retirement so that she could have sufficient opportunity to straighten out a number of matters.

'Your Honour,' Mr Isaacs continued, 'it is doubtful, after a lapse of twelve years, if any trial could be arranged earlier than 14 January, as stated by Detective McGrath. In these circumstances it would be unjust to return Mrs Gardiner immediately to South Australia,' he stated. 'Supposing she left tonight—Christmas Eve—and arrived on Monday, she would have to remain in custody from Monday to whenever the case sits.'

Ethel's barrister looked around the courtroom and again addressed the crowd. 'It will be said that this woman absconded,' he stated, pausing for effect. 'I do not shut my eyes to that, but the charge is in relation to a paltry and trivial sum of £7 13s 10d.'

He again paused, letting his statement sink in. 'Whatever her circumstances were in 1933, they are not her circumstances today. Mrs Gardiner, or as she is known properly and entitled to be known, Mrs Livesey, was granted bail of £200 when she first came to this court. She is able to secure any bail,' he concluded, before sitting himself down.

Sergeant Briese, the police prosecutor, stood to address the court. 'I ask Your Worship to take into consideration her antecedents, and refuse bail. She also absconded from bail in Adelaide for evading taxi fares.'

Mr Isaacs immediately stood: 'But that matter has been dealt with—Mrs Gardiner paid her fines in that case, did she not?' he asked the prosecutor.

'Yes,' the prosecutor reluctantly agreed.

Mr Parker looked between the two counsel. He refused the application by the Adelaide police to take Ethel in custody there and then, but increased her bond from £200 to £300, and instructed Mr Isaacs that Ethel was remanded to appear at the Adelaide Criminal Sessions of 14 January to face the charge.

Filled with relief, Ethel walked over to Mr Isaacs, shook his hand and thanked him and Mr Lander. She sauntered out of the Sydney Central Court with her legal counsel, to the cheering crowd outside.

'Thank you!' she called out to the crowd, waving as Mr Lander walked her towards the waiting car. 'Thank you one and all!'

Mrs Livesey smiling as she entered the car, paused momentarily for the photographers, and the press got their photo, which was splashed all over that evening's papers.

28

MRS LIVESEY MISSING

Ethel was besieged with letters of support. At least some people wanted to be her friends; she was gathering quite a following.

One of her new friends was a Mr James Donohue. Noting his eastern suburbs address on the letter he had sent to her via her lawyers, Ethel invited him to visit her at Mrs O'Hagan's boarding house in Chester Hill. He felt sorry for her staying in such a dilapidated house, and suggested she move into his Potts Point flat, number 10 Pembroke Hall in Macleay Street, more suitable for a lady of her standing. He also agreed to loan her £250 until funds could be sent from England, with Ethel giving him a gold cigarette case and aquamarine ring as security, together with a post-dated cheque, to be presented when the money arrived.

Ethel was back in the eastern suburbs, and immediately started writing personal replies to all the letters she had received and was still receiving, from her new upmarket address, on Mr Donohue's stationery.

Mrs Livesey was due to fly into Adelaide on 3 January with her Sydney lawyers. The South Australian press waited patiently at the airport for her plane to arrive, only to find she was not on the flight. She had disappeared again, and their newspaper columns that afternoon were filled with speculation that she'd again done a runner. Ethel had, instead, delayed her departure, as she was still trying to get in touch with her Sydney society friends.

She had managed to get in touch with Rex, via a letter, to thank him for his kind words in a newspaper article that appeared the week after their failed wedding. In the *Daily Mirror* article he explained that his feelings towards her were unchanged, that she was a marvellous woman and he held her in the highest regard. He told the reporter that he had met her when she was mixing with people in the highest society, that she had entertained lavishly, and he found her a woman of charm and personality, admitting that he'd sometimes wondered why he had been chosen as her bridegroom. When Rex replied to Ethel's thank-you letter he had been curt, saying in light of what he had found out about her since the article had been published two weeks before, he did not wish to know her.

The South Australian press then heard Mrs Livesey was to arrive on 8 January, on a flight via Melbourne. But again she didn't arrive, despite being booked on the flight, and again there were murmurings that perhaps Mrs Livesey was not going to appear at all.

But this time the reasons for Ethel's non-arrival were rather different. Ethel's notoriety had been getting her noticed everywhere, and when she had arrived in Melbourne to connect with her Adelaide flight, she had been picked up by the Victorian police, who wanted to ask her about an outstanding warrant on their books.

Two detectives questioned her in the presence of her lawyers, Messrs Isaacs and Lander, concerning a warrant issued in 1936 by a Caulfield shopkeeper, who was also brought in to verify that they had the right woman. Ethel denied she was the woman, Clara Thomas, who had passed a valueless cheque for £2 11s in his shop. She was in England at the time, married to Mr Coradine, Ethel insisted. The shopkeeper told the detectives that she *was* Clara Thomas, he wanted his money, but was finally convinced that he must have been mistaken when it was proven that she hadn't been in the country at the time.

The four hours of questioning had caused them to miss their plane. Instead, Ethel and her lawyers finally arrived in Adelaide at 9.25 that evening, to be greeted by a lone photographer who had wisely decided to see if she was on the last flight for the day. The reporters who had earlier flocked to the airport had long gone, to write columns about Mrs Livesey's latest disappearance for the evening edition of their newspapers. The patient photographer snapped a photo of Ethel emerging from the plane and rushed up to ask some questions for his unexpected scoop.

An exhausted Ethel held her hand up as he approached. 'Young man, I have had quite a day,' she began, 'I don't want to answer any questions just now.'

'Oh, I am sorry,' he began uncertainly, not used to inter-viewing, but having seen enough of it in his two short years with the paper. 'Could I perhaps come and see you tomorrow?' he asked.

The fashionably dressed Ethel stopped. 'All I ask is for a fair deal,' she said, looking the young man up and down slowly. 'I am staying at the Ambassadors. Call tomorrow and I will see how I feel—I may give you an interview,' she conceded.

'I have a story that will rock the world!'

———

The following afternoon a somewhat rested Mrs Livesey sat with the excited young photographer from the airport, together with a more seasoned reporter from the *Mirror* in the lounge of the Ambassadors Hotel, Mr Lander sitting alongside.

'I am sure that the people of Adelaide are more charitably disposed than many fairweather friends who took advantage of my hospitality in Sydney,' Ethel stated, her well-rehearsed line rippling with barely hidden anger. 'All I ask is a fair deal.'

'And what of your wedding, Mrs Livesey?' the reporter asked eagerly. 'Do you still intend to marry Mr Beech?'

'Definitely and irrevocably, no,' interjected Mr Lander.

'I do not understand why I have received so much publicity,' Ethel continued. 'It is the last thing I seek. I am not Australian by birth, but I have always understood that the great trait in the Australian nature is to give everyone, high or low, a fair deal. That is all I ask,' she repeated. 'I hope that everyone will withhold judgment of me until the court has dealt with its charge against me.'

'Your court case, will it go ahead on Monday, do you think?' the reporter asked.

Again Mr Lander interjected: 'I learned today that the Crown Prosecutor will probably seek an adjournment of the case until the February sessions, and we will of course be applying for renewed bail.'

'I see,' said the reporter to Mr Lander, 'but I understand you are unable to practise law in our state?'

'You are well informed,' Mr Lander replied. 'Yes, neither myself nor Mr Isaacs hold a licence to practise in South Australia, and we will be obtaining the services of an Adelaide solicitor, Mr Kevin Ward.'

'The police have told us that the State Children's Welfare Department wishes to speak with Mrs Livesey, seeking repayment for the care of your two sons,' the reporter noted. 'What do you have to say about that, Mrs Livesey?'

Ethel tilted her head ever so slightly at the older reporter and regarded him steadily. 'Both of my sons from a previous marriage live in Australia, and were for a time, during the Depression, under the care of the department,' she explained. 'I have every intention to pay for their keep,' she added. 'Now if you will excuse me, gentlemen, this has been a tiring few weeks and I need to rest.'

29

MRS PERCY

After that interview, on the Thursday before the trial, Ethel had been ordered by the hotel doctor to remain in bed. All meals were sent to her room, and guests were no longer permitted, her only visitors being her legal counsel Messrs Lander and Isaacs.

The doctor saw her every morning, and by Sunday, when it looked like she wouldn't be well enough to attend the trial, the judge asked for a second medical opinion. On Monday, 14 January 1946, Ethel's South Australian lawyer, Mr Ward, presented the Chief Justice with a medical certificate, the contents of which were not read out, but it was rumoured among the press that Mrs Livesey had a hernia.

It was a subdued affair in the courtroom without the glamorous figure in attendance, but the case still went ahead. It was quickly agreed that a hearing date would be set for the near future, but there was a problem: someone residing in South Australia needed to go surety for the bail, which was set at £300, as in New South Wales. Thankfully for Ethel, a good Samaritan came forward. His name was John Malcolm Doyle, and though he had never met Mrs Livesey, he had become fascinated with the newspaper stories about the cotton heiress and was in court that day. He volunteered to put up surety, saying to the press afterwards that he, like so many others, thought she'd been given a raw deal.

Ethel was free to leave South Australia and return when the prosecutor set the hearing date, with the assurance that she'd be given plenty of notice and have ample time to return.

The following day Ethel left her hotel bed, but continued to take her meals in her room.

Five days after her trial, she made her way down to the dining room in the evening after most of the other guests had left, and made her way to the piano. She sat down and entertained the few still there, including a widower, Mr Percy. Most recognised who she was and she quickly charmed her fascinated audience, sitting down and speaking with them about her life. Mr Percy stayed on and they spoke until late in the evening.

Two days later Ethel flew out of Adelaide as Mrs Percy, in name only, together with her two Sydney legal representatives. They arrived at Sydney airport at dusk—and who should be waiting there but the friendly newspaper reporter from the *Truth*.

'So lovely to see you again,' Ethel greeted him.

'It was nice of Mr Lander to tell me of your impending arrival, Mrs Percy,' he said with a grin. 'Can we have a chat?'

'I am a little tired,' she replied, 'but perhaps we could meet at my hotel later.'

The reporter watched as Mr Isaacs said farewell, and Mr Lander went to retrieve Mrs Livesey's luggage. 'How was your trip?' he asked as they waited.

'Such weather!' she exclaimed. 'I have done thousands upon thousands of miles of air travel and I really should not be scared, but you know how it is—I suppose a woman is made that way.'

'Rough trip, then?' he asked.

'I don't know how those pilots saw anything—I certainly couldn't, and it was *pouring* with rain . . . the clouds around us felt like they were tearing apart with the thunder, and the plane tossed and rolled and bucked nearly the entire trip from Melbourne!' she gasped, enjoying her story. 'But one had to only look at the broad Australian grins on the tanned faces of the pilot and co-pilot to see that there was nothing to be afraid of, and that to be in a plane in a storm was delicious fun . . . but . . . well, I didn't really enjoy rocketing through a tempest,' she enthused.

'I understand you were sick in Adelaide?' the reporter asked.

'Indeed, unfortunately I became ill,' Ethel replied. 'I thought there were some people who might have suggested that I was feigning illness, so I called in the City of Adelaide medical officer. I had three visits from him actually, and that's why I came back to Sydney, because I wanted to consult my physician here.'

'The case went ahead?' he asked.

'Yes, without me,' she said with a sigh. 'When it came before the Adelaide court the Crown authorities asked for an adjournment, so the case goes over to a future date,' she explained. 'I would of course love to discuss the case, its beginnings and its reasons, but my lawyers tell me that I am not allowed to do that.'

The reporter saw Mr Lander approaching, struggling with Mrs Livesey's baggage. Turning back to his celebrity interviewee he asked, 'I suppose you will travel by train, then, when you go back to Adelaide for the case?'

'No, certainly not!' she replied. 'I am going to fly back. That is the modern way of travel. The air, always the air.'

30

UP ON THE BIG SCREEN

Ethel sat in Mr Lander's office reading with delight the heroic recount of her plane trip across the Victorian Alps in *Truth* the following day. While the article pleased her, she was seething from her conversation with Dr Cunningham's secretary—no, Mr Cunningham could not and *would not* see Mrs Livesey, as either a patient or as a social acquaintance. He would pass her onto a colleague who could help her medically, but would appreciate it if she no longer bothered him, ever.

'Your medical records have been sent by car,' Mr Lander assured her, 'and you have an appointment with another doctor tomorrow morning at Sydney Hospital.'

'No one will see me!' Ethel complained. '*None* of them! Lady French will not even receive my calls.'

Mr Lander looked at her thoughtfully. 'Yes, well,' he began, changing the subject. 'Your newspaper articles seem to be generating the right amount of interest for us.'

'Yes, I've been thinking,' Ethel interjected. 'What do you think about recording a Cinesound newsreel to appear in the movie theatres?' she asked. 'To promote my case of course,' she added.

'If you like, Mrs Livesey,' he replied, nodding his head slowly. 'It may help your case.'

——··——

Once again her new friend Mr Donohue was called upon, this time to organise, through his contacts, a meeting with the renowned Australian director Ken Hall at Cinesound, who after meeting Mrs Livesey agreed to record a short clip for her to tell her story.

The film crew arrived at Mr Donohue's flat in Macleay Street to find the fashionable Mrs Livesey wearing her best string of pearls and large fashionable screw-on earrings, and sporting a corsage of fresh freesias and orchids on the right lapel of her sparkling black dress. They sat her down at Mr Donohue's desk with the props she had brought along—dozens of yet unopened letters of support—and set up the cameras.

As the cameras rolled, Ethel opened letter after letter, and then looked up earnestly towards the camera. 'I have taken this opportunity,' she began in the best clear-cut plummiest tone, 'to speak to the public through this medium, because what I have to say cannot be turned maliciously against me, or distorted.

'I have suffered severely in the past few weeks, through the publicity that has been given me, of which I have not sought.'

She paused for a moment, swallowed and continued on with her performance. 'I have had many hard knocks in my life, but the hardest to bear has been the mass of inactivity of people of whom I wanted their friendship most,' she said directly to the camera.

'Adversity brought me new friends,' she added, softening her tone slightly. 'Friends who I know are sincere. They come from the mass who have sympathy for a woman who is undergoing a great trial,' she paused and took a quick, angry breath, 'not the so-called Sydney society.'

She continued, 'I take this public opportunity, as the only way I can, to thank the innumerable people who have written to me. I have had more than a thousand letters. A number of them have been offering me a home and to these people I am eternally grateful. Their unselfish actions are a marked contrast to those who did not hesitate to accept my financial help, but have now excluded me from their visiting list.'

Then, looking almost directly into the camera. 'I have had a varied life, and I have seen much suffering. I went through the Blitz and the Battle of Britain. I was an air-raid warden, and I have helped on many occasions to bring out the maimed and twisted bodies from the rubble,' she paused and swallowed, closing her eyes momentarily before continuing on. 'I am very proud to have been able to have done this, because I feel as an English woman it was my duty to do so.'

She shrugged her shoulders slightly and looked angrily into the camera, her voice calm. 'Perhaps if some of those who have turned against me could have seen a little of the suffering that I have seen in the last five years of this dreadful war, they may have had a little more kindness to have shown to me in my trial,' she said, shaking her head slightly. 'I am not ashamed, of *anything* I have done, and I can look everyone in the face,' she said grimly. 'I wonder if *they* could do the same,' she stated, slapping the letter she was holding into her other hand in finality.

And so Ethel got her two minutes of fame—billed as the Cinesound Review across the country, from Friday 18 January 1946 up until her trial. For nearly a month the movie-going public across Australia watched as Ethel declared her innocence, before she was due back in Adelaide, to face the twelve-year-old charge.

31

THOUSANDS WAIT TO SEE MRS LIVESEY

Wednesday, 20 February 1946, as Mrs Livesey alighted from the back of her hire car in front of the Adelaide Criminal Court building for her first day in court, a woman suddenly rushed over and handed her a large bouquet of orchids and maiden-hair fern. The woman, a stranger, had been waiting for some time outside the court with a small baby in a pram. She almost curtsied as Ethel accepted the bouquet, to which a small card was attached. Ethel read the good wishes and thanked the young lady demurely as she turned into the court, waving as thousands in the assembled crowd outside called her name as she passed by.

The gallery was again filled with spectators as the clerk read out not one, but two charges in court. The first was to do with the Coles & Hughes drapery case; the second alleged that on 18 September 1933 she had obtained goods valued at £13 2s from the Okeh Café in Henley Beach.

Ethel stood up in court in all her finery and loudly and confidently pleaded not guilty.

The Crown Prosecutor, Mr Chamberlain, began his address to the jury, during which he referred to the 'limelight' the defendant had received, was receiving and no doubt would continue to receive. He forcefully stated that the offences were a piece of barefaced lying practised upon two innocent businesses; that the accused had been charged before a police court in 1933, and had elected herself for the case to be tried at the Criminal Court in front of a jury; and that she was committed for trial in December 1933, but had not appeared on the third day.

On the first charge, Mr Thompson, former manager of Coles & Hughes, was brought in. He glared at Ethel with open hatred as he sat down, then chose to ignore her as the prosecutor asked him to retell his story.

He stated that the accused had told him that her husband was a station owner from New South Wales and a member of the big city firm Sargood Gardiner, and he had given her goods on account as a result.

Ethel's lawyer, Mr Ward, rose and argued that the witness Mr Thompson was prepared to philander with his client. Otherwise, why else would a suburban storekeeper spend from 11.30 a.m. to 1 p.m. with her at a hotel, buying her a cocktail and then lunch?

Outraged, Mr Thompson angrily dismissed any accusation of immoral behaviour, but did eventually admit when questioned further that there had been some degree of intimacy with the woman he knew as Mrs Gardiner, as he had confided to her his troubles.

Mr Chamberlain stood and stated to the court that the accused was obviously a person of an engaging personality, as private matters were indeed openly discussed with Mr Thompson—but when detectives before the 1933 trial questioned her, she had admitted that her stories had been a myth.

On the second charge they brought in Mrs Millicent McCann, from the Okey Café. Looking nervous, Mrs McCann told them that the accused, who she knew as Mrs Anderson, had asked her for credit, stating that her husband, a magistrate, had gone to Gawler to hear a case and mistakenly taken her wallet; the accused had then come back later that same day and said her husband had been detained overnight, and she had then obtained goods on credit.

The first day of the trial ended with Mr Chamberlain repeating Milly's words: 'Mrs Gardiner's husband was *not* a magistrate, nor were the other things she supposedly told the manageress true,' he emphasised.

The following day Basil and his wife Sylvia accompanied Ethel to court. Greeted yet again by a crowd of wellwishers, Ethel smiled and waved to them as they made their way into the courthouse.

It was Ethel's turn to give her version of events. With confidence, she took the stand and in a clear, well-modulated voice stated her case: 'I am completely innocent of these two charges. I have done nothing wrong whatsoever.' She turned to the crowded courtroom and began her performance, certain that she would convince them all. 'The position was, that in 1933 I was receiving an allowance from my father in England. He used to send me £25 to £30 a month. This I would pick up at the Bank of New South Wales in Adelaide, where I also received letters. In October 1933 my allowance did not arrive. It was the Depression, and the payments could be irregular. I needed clothing for my two children,' she continued, changing the goods she purchased to something less frivolous than fancy cushions and curtains, 'and went down to the store of Coles & Hughes and asked if I might have an account. I explained about my allowance and told him I would be able to pay at the beginning of November.'

Turning to Mr Thompson, she continued, 'Mr Thompson asked me my husband's occupation and I said he was a station manager on leave. That was a fact. I told him that I had been in business in Sydney and had an account with the firm Sargood Gardiner's Sydney drapers. He then allowed me to have an account at his store and during the month I bought about £7 worth of goods, mainly for my boys.'

With barely hidden anger, she turned to the jury: 'I deny that I told him my husband was a station owner or a member of the firm Sargood Gardiner. In November 1933 I wrote to Mr Thompson and met him at the South Australia Hotel the following day and obtained the account. Two days later I was arrested,' she paused.

'After my arrest my allowance arrived and I sent the money to the firm, but Mr Thompson said the money could not be taken because the matter was out of his hands.'

Ethel looked towards the judge: 'Later, I left the money at the court. I thought that would be the end of the matter, and that was why I left Adelaide. I had every intention of paying my account, and if only the firm had been a little more patient they would have got it in person,' she remarked. The judge looked at her steadily, and she continued.

'On the second charge, Mrs McCann made a mistake,' Ethel stated. 'I told Mrs McCann that my husband had gone to the country with a *friend* who was a magistrate, and had left me short of money. That was true,' she said. 'But I went to the café a few days after and paid that account, well before I was arrested on the other charge.

'I had no intention of defrauding anyone,' Ethel continued. 'That is the whole truth. I ask you to disregard the propaganda you have read in the newspapers,' she said to the court. 'I ask you to believe me. These charges over the last few months have caused me a great deal of suffering, and I am sure you will agree they have been unnecessary. I am a sick woman.'

On the second day of the trial, Justice Mayo, the judge hearing the case, addressed the jury just before lunch asking them to consider the verdict carefully.

Four hours later the jury filed back in, with a majority verdict: the accused was *guilty* on both counts. As one, the crowd behind and above Ethel started murmuring among themselves in disbelief.

Ethel couldn't believe it herself—it was so long ago, another time, and she was a different person. She thought she had explained everything. She tried not to appear nervous as she looked at her legal team.

But there was more to come.

As the chair of the jury sat back down, Justice Mayo addressed the court as the crowd voluntarily shushed to listen. 'There are various aspects to be considered,' he began. 'My present idea is that I will have to sentence her to some term of imprisonment, but I want to look at it all ways.'

Ethel looked desperately at the judge and back again to her three lawyers, two of whom had not been allowed to address the court. Justice Mayo then asked both the prosecutor, Mr Chamberlain, and Ethel's solicitor, Mr Ward, for comment.

'Your Honour,' Mr Ward appealed, 'Mrs Gardiner made restitution at the time in both cases, paying the money she owed to the Okey Café, and in the Coles & Hughes case the account payment was made to the police court. I have been instructed by my client that there existed a police docket bearing a note to that effect—can it not be sought?'

Justice Mayo thought for a moment, then turned to address the prosecutor. 'Have you come across this note?'

'No, Your Honour,' Mr Chamberlain stated, 'but I will undertake to do so now.'

Justice Mayo looked at him with a small level of contempt. 'You can let me know in the morning. I shall have to consider.

I think it is a mistake to deal with these cases in haste. If I see my way clear not to imprison her, I will not.'

———·——

Basil and Sylvia were again waiting for her, when Ethel arrived back at court under police escort the following day, Friday 22 February 1946, still unsure whether she would be sent to prison. It was a hot summer's day, and she'd spent the previous night in the lock-up and was not looking quite as groomed as she normally did. The evening papers had been filled with her guilty verdict, and while there was a crowd both inside and outside the courthouse, there were no flowers nor words of encouragement. Just looks of silent, curious and occasionally hostile stares.

Justice Mayo started by asking Mr Chamberlain whether he had been able to locate the police docket showing the Coles & Hughes money being repaid.

'No, Your Honour,' he began. 'But, I have received yet further information which I did not have at hand yesterday. On top of the defendant's two convictions, Mrs Gardiner had a conviction in the name of Gloria Grey,' he paused, looking at Ethel momentarily before continuing. 'Under that name she was found guilty of false pretences in Melbourne in June 1934, for which she received six months gaol.'

The gallery erupted with murmurings that grew louder.

The judge banged his gavel down and glared at the public gallery.

Ethel's three legal representatives, Messrs Lander, Isaacs and Ward, were all silently staring at her; she looked back at them blankly before returning her attention to the judge.

Mr Chamberlain was waving a docket in his hand. 'I have a minute here, of the late Detective Trezona who handled the case,' he began, 'dated December 5, 1933, that on the 4th of December the defendant had not returned to her residence. I have no further instructions about restitution being paid to Coles & Hughes, and in the absence of anyone to whom it could now be made, may I suggest that Your Honour ignore it.'

Justice Mayo nodded thoughtfully, then turned to Ethel.

'In sentencing, I am not clear what the defendant's name really is. In these proceedings she has been shown to have used the names Grey, Gardiner and Anderson.'

'That's the name!' yelled a young man from the gallery. 'Her name is Anderson!'

'Remove anyone who makes a noise, Sergeant,' Justice Mayo yelled above the noisy public gallery as everyone started trying to see who had made the remark.

'Her name is Anderson,' the young man repeated loudly and clearly.

Ethel along with everyone in the courtroom was staring up into the crowded public gallery, and her eyes locked on to those of her long lost son, Frank George Anderson. He was staring down at her, his eyes cold and steady as two court officials fought their way through the packed gallery to evict him.

'These charges,' Justice Mayo continued as Frank was led away, 'could have been disposed of summarily in November 1933 had the defendant herself not chosen—as she was entitled to do—to be tried by a jury.

'My impression,' he stated, looking directly at Ethel, 'which might be unfounded, was that that choice was not unconnected with a decision to appear at trial.'

He cleared his throat and continued on. 'She did not appear to her recognisance, but I understand from her counsel that she has since paid the amounts owed. Over twelve years have elapsed since the offences, and her past record is not clear.'

Ethel did not move as he regarded her carefully. 'I have no information as to where she has been since 1934, but there is nothing to indicate any infraction of the criminal law, and I accept her record as clear since then.'

Ethel's shoulders visibly relaxed, and she turned as Mr Chamberlain moved in his chair and glared at Ethel and her legal team.

Justice Mayo then addressed Ethel directly. 'These offences are serious. Preying on the community by fraud must be suppressed. You are getting on in years and your state of health is serious,' he told her. 'You have ability and astuteness, undoubtedly, but I think you may also have some extreme form of egotism.

'It might well be that if the police court had dealt with the matter, the order might have been similar to that which I now propose,' observed Justice Mayo, looking around the court. 'The publicity which has been given to the case should not alter the penalty.

'Mrs Gardiner,' he said, again addressing Ethel.

Mr Lander turned and gestured for her to stand, which she did uncertainly; Sylvia rose alongside and helped her as she seemed to sway.

'I have decided that it is not necessary to impose imprisonment at present. You will pay a bond of £300, with a surety of £300, to be of good behaviour for three years,' he pronounced, looking at her intently, 'and you are to notify the police of your address, or any changes of address, whenever you might be in South Australia in that period.'

With that, a slightly stunned-looking Ethel was free to leave.

———————

The day after the trial, Ethel was at her son Basil's house, in Holbrooks Road, Flinders Park. It was decided that she would stay with him and his wife Sylvia for a few days.

Frank, now 21, and who had not seen his mother for twelve long years, was also there. Having seen news of the trial splashed over all the newspapers, he wanted to know the truth about all these fantastic stories of his mother, and to know why she had deserted him and Basil as young boys.

Ethel had been reliving stories of her past with Frank and Basil—or her versions of them, at least—trying to justify her abandonment of them, insisting there had never been a day she hadn't thought of them. Basil was quite forgiving, having been gifted a newsagency business by Ethel, but Frank was rather bitter: how could she have left them to foster care, while she herself was living so lavishly? Why hadn't she come looking for them?

At 2 p.m. that afternoon, a reporter from the *Mail* knocked on the door to interview Ethel.

Ethel placed her swollen feet on the hassock in front of her chair with a sigh. 'My son's home has become such a sanctuary for me,' she told the reporter.

'Tell me, Mrs Livesey, how do you feel about the trial verdict?'

'I cannot speak too highly of my legal advisors—Messrs Isaacs and Ward,' she began. 'My conviction was a gross miscarriage of justice,' her eyes flashing in barely concealed anger, though her voice was calm. 'And I have suffered much. They even put me in gaol overnight! I have suffered a terrible ordeal.'

'How did you find that, Mrs Livesey, being in gaol?' he asked, madly taking notes.

'Considering it a place of punishment, remarkably hospitable and clean,' she replied. 'The wardresses were the acme of kindness, and the blankets were as good as some I have had in many of the best hotels.'

'And the prison food, is it as bad as they say?' the reporter asked.

'I cannot comment on the meals, as I felt too ill to eat, and I did not sleep well. I have not been sleeping or eating well for some time,' she admitted. 'And as for these dreadful reports in some of the papers, saying I am nineteen stone!' she said, raising her voice. 'Obviously a *misprint* as I weigh only fourteen stone seven pounds!' Her two boys looked at each other, Frank raising his eyebrows at his brother, which Ethel saw and attempted to ignore. Stone-faced, she took an angry sip of her whiskey and placed it back on the table beside her.

'You have received plenty of support as a result of your coverage, I understand?' the reporter asked.

'People have been so kind,' Ethel replied. 'Complete strangers writing to me. Since my conviction I have received over 1000 letters of sympathy, many offers of accommodation and homes, and numerous gifts of flowers—all of which I appreciate immensely.'

'Do you intend to stay in South Australia?'

'Now that the trial is over, once I am feeling rested, I intend to return to Sydney, where I anticipate many interesting interviews with people whom I lavishly entertained, and who, in my hour of need, deserted me,' her blue eyes again flashing in anger.

'Many of my so-called Sydney friends forsook me without hearing me!' she stated again, raising her voice slightly. 'I have spent *thousands* on entertaining Sydney society—and yet, with a few exceptions, these people have abandoned me. I spent £250 on the wedding reception, and that did not include drinks. Then almost everyone forsook me because of something they had heard about me!'

She paused again, then declared dramatically: 'I am writing a book on my life. Two publishing houses are interested—my story will rock Australia, I can promise you that, and it gets better as the years go by. Tell me,' she asked the reporter, 'have you seen the newsreel I was in?'

'It was hard to miss,' he muttered.

'Yes well, Ken Hall—the Australian film director, you may have heard of him—he wants to make my story into a film.'

'That would be interesting. What name would you go by, what is your *real* name?' the reporter asked.

Ethel burred visibly. 'My name is *Livesey*. It was changed by deed poll, owing to family reasons. That can be proved by gazette.'

'And I see both your sons are with you. I understand they were put into the care of the state's Children's Welfare Department?'

'It was an unfortunate time, the Depression,' Ethel replied, 'but I have paid over £300 for their maintenance. Some years ago, I even disguised myself as a nun and came here, going from school to school, trying to find my boys,' she stated, the boys again looking at each other, but this time in surprise. 'When I returned from England last August, I came first to Adelaide to see them. I found Basil, and Frank here just recently,' she replied looking over towards her son, 'he has been travelling.'

Wrapping up the interview, Ethel rose to see the reporter to the door.

'The past is behind me,' she told him. 'I look to the future with confidence.'

32

GOING FOR BROKE

And so Ethel moved back to Sydney, and was welcomed into Mrs O'Hagan's boarding house once again. Her main aim was to attempt to redress the damage to her reputation and the many so-called injustices heaped upon her by her former society friends. Instead, she was surprised to receive from her solicitor Mr Lander additional bills for the wedding that never was.

While she had been 'sick' in January before the Adelaide trial, Civic Hire Services had served her with a writ for money owed for hire cars for her wedding—£114 6s (over $7000). She thought she'd managed to get out of the fee by being 'friendly' with the owner, but clearly his angry wife had thought otherwise, she was taking Ethel to court on behalf of their company.

In early March, she went to Mr Lander's office, only to also be presented with a bill for their legal work—£1910 18s 5d (over $120,000). She'd already paid them over £1000, in cash!

Ethel stormed out of Mr Lander's chambers at 79 Elizabeth Street, went next door to number 81 and hired another lawyer, Harold Munro.

Mr Munro happily greeted his infamous client and listened to her woes. She was running out of money she claimed—she had funds coming to her from England, from the sale of some property, but she had little until it arrived. She had spent a fortune on the wedding that had never happened, and someone had suggested she go after her former fiancé, Rex Beech, for breach of promise. She asked Mr Munro to start the process.

When it became known she was taking Mr Beech to court, the newspapers once again had a field day, reliving the wedding that never was, the story of the guilty heiress, and now a £10,000 (just over $600,000) lawsuit. The public gobbled it up, especially when it was reported that Mr Beech only earned about £7 a week working at the Treasury.

Ethel's court cases provided juicy pickings for the newspapers.

First up came the car-hire case, in the District Court. Ethel lost the case and was ordered to pay the bill for £114 6s, plus £12 12s in court costs.

Next was a case for her large outstanding account for the supply of alcohol. At the beginning of April, Ivan St Clair, owner of the Double Bay company Household Supply took her to court for the £149 8s 7d ($9000) she owed. His company had provided alcohol to Mrs Livesey before the wedding and for the reception, and it still hadn't been paid for. At this second case, it was reported that Ethel was suddenly too ill to attend court; her solicitor, Mr Munro, apologised to the judge for her absence, then said he thought it a matter for settlement rather than litigation, and that the account would be paid when his client was feeling better.

A few days later, a small article reported that Mrs Gardiner had paid the outstanding surety of £50 from the 1933 case in Adelaide when she'd absconded from her trial; the fact she'd finally paid the South Australian Government £300 for child welfare also made the papers. She was trying to clean up her past.

———•••———

Then came the breach of promise case, in the Supreme Court of New South Wales, on Friday, 17 May, 1946.

Mr Munro had organised two legal colleagues—barrister and doctor of letters Dr Frank Louat, and barrister Mr Alan Bagot—to attend court with himself and Mrs Livesey.

Ethel's former friend Mac—or Mr G.R.W. McDonald, as he was introduced to the court—was acting for Rex Beech, and seated beside them was their barrister, Mr John Leaver.

Mac and Mr Beech glared at her when she entered the court-room with her legal team. She attempted a smile at them both, but in unison they turned away.

She sat herself down and looked across at them, hoping to catch Rex's eye, but he steadfastly ignored her.

Dr Louat rose to state Ethel's case. 'Mrs Livesey and Mr Beech agreed to marry on the 8th of December, 1945,' he began, his rich, mellow voice booming around the courtroom.

'Mrs Livesey had always been ready and willing, and although a reasonable amount of time has elapsed, Mr Beech has refused to marry her, injuring her feelings,' he said, turning towards his client and then back to the court, 'as well as causing her to sustain considerable financial loss.'

'I see,' replied Mr Justice Owen. 'And how do you come to this figure of £10,000?'

'We will argue that Mrs Livesey lent Mr Beech considerable amounts of money, which we wish to have returned, as well as payment of money received by Mr Beech on her behalf, and reimbursement of funds spent, gifts totalling £895, and an additional £127 spent in preparation for the marriage— together with damages for the loss of Mrs Livesey's reputation and emotional hardship.'

'Very well,' the judge murmured. 'Mr McDonald?' he said, looking over towards Mac and Mr Beech.

'Your Honour,' replied Mac, rising to his feet. 'Mr Beech would like to plead a general denial to allegations of breach of promise, and the indebtedness, and as a third plea that he made the promise of marriage believing she was a chaste and modest woman, where she had not always been and was not.'

This remark brought about a murmuring in the press gallery—more dirt for their columns.

Justice Owen looked over to them sharply, then turned back to Mr McDonald.

'Our fourth plea is that Mr Beech was induced to make the promise by misrepresentation and wilful suppression by Mrs Livesey of the real circumstances of her family and previous life, which he discovered after making the promise,' Mac stated.

He took a moment and cleared his throat. 'Your Honour, the fifth plea is that Mr Beech made the promise in faith of the statement by Mrs Livesey that she was a widow of a wealthy and reputable man, Mr James Livesey, who had been killed in a bomb raid in London, whereas the fact was that the plaintiff had for some years—until her recent departure from England— been living with the said man James Livesey, then a married man, which the defendant first discovered after making the alleged promise.'

Those in the press gallery were scribbling frantically—this would certainly sell a few papers!

Mr Munro stood up and addressed the court.

'Your Honour, we ask that Mr Beech detail particulars of his allegations of acts of unchastity or immodesty, and of the alleged wilful misrepresentations and suppressions,' he stated. 'And we ask for a withdrawal of the first plea—the general denial of breach of promise—and the fifth—the allegation of adultery—on the ground that they are embarrassing to my client, and of a kind that would defeat or delay the proper trial of the action.'

Mac looked over at Ethel with disdain as he rose to answer Munro. 'As to the fourth plea—particulars of the alleged misrepresentations,' he said to court, 'they are many.'

And he proceeded to list them: 'That she was an heiress related to the Coats family controlling large cotton interests; that she was the owner of a controlling interest in Courtaulds, the British rayon firm; that she owned a magnificent château in Monte Carlo; that she owned large and elaborate homes in the Isle of Man, Wales and Torquay; and that she employed large staffs of servants.

'That she held rent-producing properties in London, Liverpool and Manchester; that she was the owner of an elaborate yacht on which she entertained the Duke of Windsor and his friends; and that she is the possessor of freehold and share interests in England and America, which produced income that—even after paying exorbitant amounts of tax—left her with enough for lavish living and large charitable gifts . . . '

Mac paused for effect. 'All of these are misrepresentations,' he concluded.

Dr Louat rose. 'In regard to this fourth plea—the alleged misrepresentations—there is no legal authority for the raising by a man of such matters as a defence to a breach of promise suit,' he said, looking at the judge. 'All they amount to is that Mr Beech was disappointed because he discovered he was not marrying into the wealth he thought he was, but there was no reason for him breaking his promise of marriage.'

'I should have thought it was,' Justice Owen replied. 'Do you mean to say that if a man represented to a woman that he was wealthy and so on, and then she found out that he wasn't, she would be entitled to refuse to marry him?' he asked.

'That would be so in the case of a *woman*,' Dr Louat replied, 'because though a man is responsible for maintaining the wife, a wife is not responsible for maintaining her husband. I submit the positions are not reversible.'

Mr Beech's barrister, Mr Leaver, then rose and addressed the court. 'We wish to make amendments to the first, fourth and fifth pleas if it pleases Your Honour,' he said.

'I will strike them out,' Justice Owen remarked, making a note on the papers in front of him, 'and give you seven days to amend them. Mr Beech is to pay costs.'

As they went to leave the courthouse, the reporter from the *Sydney Morning Herald* saw Mr Leaver turn to Mac and state loudly enough for most to hear, 'This may prove to be the most frivolous action ever conceived in these courts!'

The press had what they wanted. Even though Mrs Livesey had failed to get money out of Mr Beech this time, they had even more juicy personal details about the supposed cotton heiress, perfect for the evening news.

———••———

Mac was kept busy. As well as defending Mr Beech, he was also acting for Mr St Clair, who had provided the alcohol for Ethel's planned wedding. The case was being put before the Federal Bankruptcy Court due to the continued lack of payment.

Ethel left Mr Munro to face Justice Thomas Clyne alone.

'We would like an adjournment for fourteen days,' Mr Munro told the court at the opening of the hearing on Friday, 31 May. 'My client is again in Adelaide, ill, and I cannot get instructions.' He then read an affidavit stating that before she left for Adelaide, she had told him she intended to undergo a serious operation.

He went on to say she had questioned a single item on the account for £75 (nearly $4500) listed as 'money expended for goods delivered'. According to Mac, her previous lawyer Mr Lander had received advice from Mr St Clair that it was for French liqueurs supplied at the special request of Mrs Livesey for the wedding.

'We never handled those liqueurs,' Mr Munro stated. 'They were supposed to be delivered to my client's flat, but were taken away by a man named Beech and she doesn't know what was delivered, and she does not know what she has to pay for. This woman did purchase certain liqueurs in contemplation of an impending marriage to Beech. The wedding fell through, and this man Beech and his associates drank these liqueurs, while she was away weeping somewhere else, and she has never seen them,' he ended dramatically.

'What have you to say about this, Mr McDonald?' Justice Clyne asked.

Mac rose carefully from his seat. 'My friend is slightly amiss, I think, in regard to the facts—particularly in relation to the last item, because I am in a position to know that Mr Beech did not consume or remove them,' he stated.

'I submit that the application for this adjournment is not bona fide at all; it is simply intended to delay sequestration of the judgment. On the 21st December I understand the debtor was arrested on a charge of false pretences and granted bail to appear in Adelaide. She left New South Wales, leaving the debt unpaid.

'In regard to the illness,' Mac continued confidently, 'there is no evidence or information in support of the fact that she suffers from this malady—and it is noticeable from the press reports that this malady she suffers from seems to occur when she is required in one of our courts.

'I say that this application is filed now for no other purpose than to delay the petitioner. It is a fact known to me—which I could put in an affidavit—that my client is not the only victim.'

'I do not think you should say that,' Mr Munro replied directly to Mac.

'I am speaking very advisedly,' Mac replied steadily. 'But perhaps I should not have said that.'

Justice Clyne looked at the two lawyers for a moment. 'I will not grant the adjournment, Mr Munro,' he decided. He turned to Mac and asked the particulars of the bankruptcy notice, before making an order of sequestration, where the Official Receiver—a Mr Richardson—could seek and seize any assets to pay the creditor.

The press reporters now had even more dirt on the absent Mrs Livesey, and publicised her apparent financial downfall with glee: Mrs Florence Elizabeth Ethel Livesey—one of the most lavish entertainers ever to startle Sydney society into a stampede for places in the free champagne queue— was bankrupt.

33

MRS LIVESEY AGAIN MISSING

On Wednesday, 3 July 1946, a total of nine creditors attended a meeting with the Official Receiver, Mr Richardson.

Mr Richardson had to advise them that Mrs Livesey had not been served with the order of sequestration of her estate, because she could not be found, and as a result had not filed the required statement of financial affairs, and as a result the court did not know how much money she was worth.

However, his enquiries had found Mrs Livesey did still own two investment properties in England—59 Hope Street and 146 Chatlam Street in Liverpool—together said to be worth £1250 (over $78,000). The creditors unanimously agreed that these properties be sold at auction without reserve, which would at least cover some of the money owed.

The meeting adjourned with Richardson advising the

creditors to seek their own legal counsel while the Bankruptcy Court undertook to find the elusive Mrs Livesey.

———··———

Sergeant McGrath and Officer Eyles from the Adelaide CIB visited Basil's home to ask if he knew of his mother's whereabouts. Basil was at work, so they spoke with his wife Sylvia instead.

'So where is Mrs Livesey?' Officer Eyles asked her. It had been his job during the war to interview German nationals prior to internment, and he was used to getting answers.

'I don't know. Truly, I don't,' she sighed. 'She left six or seven weeks ago.'

'Where was she headed?' he demanded.

'I don't know,' Sylvia replied. 'I think she was going to Victoria, but I don't know where.'

'Come now Mrs Anderson, you put up her £300 bond five months ago, and you really don't know where she has gone?'

Sylvia looked at him in alarm. 'Will I have to pay the bond?' she asked urgently. 'She hasn't done anything wrong, has she? I mean, I really don't know *where* she has gone, or when she's coming back, or *anything*! We can't afford to lose that much money—*any* money.'

'Perhaps you should have thought about that when you put the bond up,' he replied.

Syliva looked like she was about to burst into tears.

'Do you know if she has any money here?' he asked.

Sylvia again shook her head. 'I think she's broke,' she replied. 'In fact the way she carried on in this house, I'm sure she *is* broke, but she is a woman that will tell you nothing about her finances, so actually I don't know.'

Justice Clyne was getting frustrated. Despite certified letters being sent all over the country to known addresses used by Mrs Livesey, they weren't getting what they were after—her necessary statement of affairs. The court had, however, received an affidavit from her returning most of the documentation, everything except the statement of affairs. They had no idea how much money she had, and she wasn't telling them.

'I think we had better fix a date for the Committal Hearing,' he said to Mr Richardson. 'Perhaps the threat of prison will bring her forward.'

The Official Receiver gave a nod. 'I fear that this bankrupt may have money at her disposal which she may be using,' he replied. 'A letter arrived from her late last Friday, but I didn't see it until Monday,' he said handing it to Justice Clyde.

The judge looked it over and turned the envelope over in his hand. 'This letter seems to suggest that she is in Melbourne; it is fairly clear that she is no longer in Adelaide. What is this postmark on the envelope? "A.L.B." or "A.L.D."?'

'I think that it is probably Algate, which is about 25 miles from Adelaide, and I have formed the opinion that the letter was posted on the Melbourne train,' Richardson replied.

'That is a rather curious thing, why was it not posted from Melbourne if that is where the letter states she is?' Clyde asked.

'She may desire to get a postmark shown at some place other than Melbourne or Adelaide,' Richardson replied.

Justice Clyne, tapping the envelope in his hand, pondered for a long moment. 'What is it you suggest doing?' he asked.

'Advertise the committal in the major evening papers in each state,' Mr Richardson replied.

'If it was put on the front page among the cables, she would probably see it then,' Justice Clyne agreed, making a note. 'Can you suggest anything else?' He watched as the tired receiver went through his papers, and finding what he was after, held it before him.

'Mr Munro was her solicitor, but he has told me he is now no longer acting for her; he sent me a list of fifteen creditors seeking Mrs Livesey, but he did not know her present address,' Mr Richardson explained. 'I do not think it effective to send a notice to Mr Munro, but it may be useful to have papers sent to Mrs Sylvia Anderson in Adelaide; she probably feels that she has been worried too much by her husband's mother's affairs. And may I also suggest a notice be served to the manager of the Bank of New South Wales head office in Melbourne, where we know she last withdrew money.'

'Very well,' Justice Clyne declared. 'On this day, the 2nd of August 1946, I order the bankrupt Florence Elizabeth Ethel Livesey to appear before the Bankruptcy Court in Melbourne on Monday, 19 August 1946 at 10.30 a.m., or an order for the committal of the said bankrupt to prison on the grounds of her failure to observe the obligations imposed under the Bankruptcy Act will be issued.'

'Mrs Livesey!'

Mr Herbert Wheatley addressed Ethel in the reception area of his legal firm, where a clerk and secretary had been trying not to look at her too obviously as she waited.

'Won't you come into my office? This way,' he smiled, indicating his room.

He closed the door behind them, showing her to a chair opposite his desk.

'What can I do for you today?' he asked.

'Well Mr Wheatley, I am not sure if you are aware, but I have had a dreadful time lately,' Ethel began.

'I have been following the papers a little, Mrs Livesey.'

'Well then, you know of some of my troubles. But it was only this morning that I read *this* in the paper, and I am unsure what to do,' she said quietly, holding the front page of the *West Australian* towards him, and pointing to the notice of committal against her. 'I seek your expertise.'

At breakfast that morning, Mr Wheatley had already read about the bankruptcy motion and threatened committal against the notorious lady sitting opposite. He looked carefully at his potential new client.

'Why did you come to Western Australia, Mrs Livesey?' he enquired. 'You must excuse me, but was it to avoid the Bankruptcy Court?'

'Certainly not!' she declared, then in a calmer tone continued, 'I came some weeks ago, seeking some respite from the strain to which I have been subjected through the continuous publicity given to my affairs. Particularly after the

South Australian court case, I felt like I was on the verge of a breakdown, and was continually worried.'

She explained that the court cases had left her with very little money, and that she had been in search of work. 'I managed to gain a domestic position in Melbourne,' she told him, 'but as soon as they found out who I was, they threw me out! I came to this state in an endeavour to live and work quietly.'

Pausing, she added: 'I have been in ill health for some time, Mr Wheatley. On the journey over by train I stayed nearly the entire time in bed, and I am still unwell. I am greatly concerned that I would not survive the journey back, but if I must appear before a court in the eastern states, I will endeavour to do so.'

The lawyer nodded in understanding. 'We can obtain a medical certificate for you, Mrs Livesey; I will arrange a consultation with a friend of mine after our meeting. But in the meantime, we will need to go through the requirements for the Bankruptcy Court. Now tell me,' he said, picking up a pen and taking notes on the legal pad in front of him, 'do you remember receiving documentation from the Official Receiver?'

'Why yes, my lawyer in Adelaide, Mr Ward, sent me a series of forms, which I dutifully filled out and returned by post,' she replied.

'There should have been a statement of affairs in which you state your known assets and liabilities. Do you remember filling that out, by chance?' he asked.

'I think so,' Ethel replied a little uncertainly. 'They have confiscated my accounts; I cannot withdraw any funds.

I have little more than a few pounds in cash, Mr Wheatley—enough to pay your fee,' she added reassuringly, 'but they claim I withdrew large sums of money from the Isle of Man prior to coming to this country, and I have no clue as to where this fable came from.'

'You deny this?' he asked, looking across at her.

'Emphatically!' she replied.

'I see,' he said quietly. 'I will write to them today and ask what the nature of the proceedings are at present before the court, and we will see what we can do.'

'Please make it abundantly clear to them, Mr Wheatley, that I will give them all the information that they require, but I do fear I will not make the journey back. And I cannot go to prison.'

34

WHERE DID ALL THE MONEY GO?

On Monday, 19 August, the Honourable Mr Justice Clyne was seated in the Victorian Court of Bankruptcy in Melbourne, expecting to interview Mrs Livesey.

Mr Richardson, the Official Receiver, held some informative documents for him instead.

The first was a letter from Wheatley & Son, solicitors in Perth, dated 5 August 1946, together with a medical certificate stating that Mrs Livesey was unable to travel.

The second was a letter from a Mr D.A. Alexander, Deputy Director of the Criminal Investigation Branch in Melbourne, outlining some interesting information from the Criminal Investigation Department of New Scotland Yard: enquiries made to certain banks—including the Isle of Man Bank, where Mrs Livesey had an account—suggested she withdrew large amounts prior to her departure to Australia. Bank records then traced to Australia showed deposits amounting to £23,656 (just under $1.5 million) between 27 August 1945 and January 1946.

This last revelation caused quite a stir in the packed press gallery: how could someone having received that much money, in less than six months, be in a bankruptcy court?

The third document was an application for a search warrant, also sent by Mr Alexander of Melbourne CIB, for a rural property at Weering, in Victoria. Police had been notified that Mrs Livesey had worked as a housekeeper for two elderly brothers and their sister for some weeks before the publicity caught up with her; Mrs Livesey had then left for Perth, leaving undisclosed belongings in a locked room on the property.

Justice Clyne approved the search warrant application, and the matter was adjourned.

The press gallery exited quickly, eager once again to fill their columns with the latest on Mrs Livesey, and the tantalising possibility of a treasure trove in a locked room in rural Victoria.

The week following, Justice Clyne perused the documentation in front of him. Unfortunately for the creditors, the only item of immediate monetary value recovered from the search of Mrs Livesey's goods on the Weering property was one solid gold bangle. He let out a sigh.

He did have some good news, however: the CIB in Melbourne had Mrs Livesey's passport and had asked the Customs Department not to furnish her with another, giving them descriptions and photographs of the wanted woman. She couldn't leave the country.

———···———

At the next court sitting, Justice Clyne was presented with an affidavit from Mr Wheatley, Ethel's Perth lawyer, together with the all-important statement of affairs.

In the assets column was the Liverpool real estate, valued at £1250, and cash in hand of £20. She listed ten unsecured creditors she owed money to, totalling £1307, and two additional 'secured' creditors: Mr B. Johnson of the Australia Hotel, to whom she had given a silver-and-gold toilet set as security for a £100 loan; and Mr Donohue, who had helped her find a flat in Sydney's eastern suburbs, giving him a cigarette case and her aquamarine diamond engagement ring as security for his £200 loan.

She also stated she had drawn no more than £4000 from her overseas accounts—and yet according to the same statement, had managed to pay out more than £7000 since arriving in Australia: £1650 in solicitor fees to Mr Lander, £350 to Child Welfare, £240 in rent, £350 on the wedding that didn't happen, £200 for presents to Mr Beech, £150 sent to her father as well as a gift of £2000, £200 for her fare to Australia, £125 to Mr Livesey as a gift, £200 in rent for the Isle of Man property, £185 in debts paid on the Isle of Man, and only £60 on living expenses and entertainment since she had arrived. According to her statement, she'd spent £7437 in twelve months, not £23,656.

Justice Clyne looked at the list and immediately two questions came to mind. How could she spend almost double what she stated she withdrew from her accounts? And, what about the rest of the £23,656—did she have it hidden away?

He placed the statement of affairs to one side and looked at the woman's affidavit. She was living in Victory Flats, 90 Bulwer Street, East Perth. She claimed she had lost her job in Melbourne and travelled to Perth in a bad nervous condition, only aware of the committal proceedings from a notice in the *West Australian* newspaper on 5 August, having left everything in the hands of her Sydney solicitor, Mr Harry Munro. Her only prospect of continuing in employment to support herself was to stay in Western Australia where there was less publicity, she stated, and that she was still unable to travel due to her health.

Justice Clyne contemplated both documents.

After some deliberation, he decided to withdraw the committal order on Mrs Livesey, as the imminent sale of her properties in England would almost cover the creditors on her list.

It was up to those creditors not on her list to prove their debt to the court, meaning more delays.

For the meantime, he ruled, she was free to stay in Perth.

———

On Tuesday, 8 October, Rex Beech waited in court for the rescheduled breach of promise case with Mac and their legal team in Sydney.

They waited in vain. The court had ordered Mrs Livesey to set the matter down for trial, but she had failed to do so.

Her name was read out three times inside and outside the court, and she did not appear.

The judgment was signed in Mr Beech's favour, with Mrs Livesey to pay costs.

35

GOING AFTER THE LAWYERS

In October, a creditors' meeting was also held in Sydney. Mr Richardson, the Official Receiver, looked at the assembled creditors, from business people to a frail elderly lady, and wondered how he was going to break this to them. Straight out, he decided.

'The two properties Mrs Livesey owns are worth much less than was claimed,' he started.

Immediately everyone wanted to talk at once. How come? What happened? Were the properties dilapidated?

He looked at them steadily and continued. 'Not because the properties are inferior,' he assured them, 'but because both have long–term leases in place, for 75 years each.'

Of all the properties Ethel had acquired from the late Mr Coradine, Mr Livesey and her father, these were the two she had been unable to sell off quickly, and this had been the reason why.

'The lease on the Chatham Street property is due to expire in November 1952,' he continued.

'But that is over *six years* away!' Mr St Clair stated.

Mr Richardson nodded and continued reading from the paper in front of him. 'And the Hope Street property lease won't be completed until September 1976.'

The creditors seemed momentarily stunned—that was *three decades* away!

The elderly woman in the front row started to sob. Even though Mrs Sarah Stanbury was the smallest creditor, Mr Richardson's heart went out to her. Mrs Stanbury had apparently written to Mrs Livesey back in December, offering her support, and the woman had landed on their doorstep less than a month later. She and her husband had lent her the £10 they had saved for their funeral costs, without security. But as Mrs Stanbury hadn't been on Mrs Livesey's statement of affairs, the chances of getting their money back was slim. To top it off, all the stress had sent her husband to bed, ill, and Mrs Stanbury was worried, as now she had no savings. If her husband passed away, she would be unable to pay for his funeral.

Another of the creditors, Miss Nicholson, herself out of pocket £70, was trying to console the old lady.

'So, the properties are worthless!' Mr St Clair fumed.

'No, Mr St Clair, they are still generating a small amount of rent, which is going to the bankrupt estate—but, I'm afraid, not many people will be interested in purchasing them at this stage,' Mr Richardson replied. 'So they may have to be sold for considerably less.'

'How much less?' Mr St Clair demanded.

'According to the agent in the UK, we could hope to net approximately £200 in total, if a buyer can be found.'

'That is outrageous!'

Mr Richardson looked at the agitated man standing before him and decided to lay it on the line.

'All secured creditors, those like yourself Mr St Clair, who have proof of debt, will have first priority of payment from the estate as a percentage of how much the estate is worth in total— which at this stage, if what Mrs Livesey has told us is correct, looks like being not worth much more than £400, including what we seized from her bank accounts and will generate from the sale of her jewellery on hand.'

'And, what about those of us with unsecured loans?' Miss Nicholson asked.

'I'm afraid the chances of securing funds are limited, unless Mrs Livesey has seen fit to place you on her statement of affairs as a debtor, which I understand she has with you Miss Nicholson.'

'But, not me?' Mrs Stanbury said quietly.

'No,' Mr Richardson replied, his heart sinking as the old lady's face fell into her hands and she sobbed quietly.

Mr Richardson paused, unsure how the creditors would receive his next piece of news.

'I have here a letter from Mr Livesey, saying he will pay £100 for the Chatham Street property, and £50 for the Hope Street property, from the bankrupt estate.'

'Mr Livesey?' Mr St Clair asked. 'The husband, or partner, or whatever he is?'

'Yes.'

'Can we claim off him?'

'No,' Mr Richardson said, suppressing a sigh. 'He is not the bankrupt in this case, and they were not legally man and wife.'

The creditors were momentarily quiet, before Mr St Clair broke the silence. 'Well then, what about all that money paid to those solicitors of hers? Half of the people here lent her money to pay *them*—it was a *ridiculous* amount! Could we get *that* money back some way?'

'Possibly,' Mr Richardson replied cautiously. 'You could ask the courts to vet the lawyers' bill of costs, and if they are not satisfied with the fees charged, there may be some refunded.' This caused a stir among the creditors.

'Can we,' Mr Richardson entreated, trying to get their attention again, 'can we deal with Mr Livesey's offer first?'

'A hundred and fifty pounds!' Mr St Clair spluttered. 'For two properties supposed to be worth nearly *ten* times that amount—I don't think so!'

'They are only worth what someone is willing to pay,' Mr Richardson pointed out patiently.

'I say we go after the lawyers!' urged Mr St Clair. 'Who's with me?' There was a general murmuring among the creditors that was growing louder. 'Show of hands then!' he shouted. Each of the creditors raised a hand.

'So what is it that you agree upon?' Mr Richardson asked in exasperation. 'To not accept Mr Livesey's offer?'

'Not accept Livesey's offer!' reiterated Mr St Clair. 'And go after the lawyers.'

———·•·———

Mr Lander, Ethel's former Sydney lawyer, refused consent to having his account reviewed—until an order was issued by the Supreme Court on 20 November 1946.

Appearing before Mr Justice Maxwell on 22 November, Mr Lander stated at the start of the hearing: 'I do not oppose the application, Your Honour. I submit that this is the proper stage for the court to decide whether Mrs Livesey had been adequately advised.'

Justice Maxwell then ordered that Mr Lander's three bills of costs be referred to the taxing master to deal with.

All day they nitpicked through the bills, questioning numerous seemingly large charges for phone calls to Randwick Racecourse to leave urgent messages for Mr Isaacs, large fees for dealing with the press, for not getting home before 11 p.m., and non-professional charges such as having to purchase airline tickets and send telegrams. The area that drew the most argument was the huge sums paid to Messrs Isaacs and Lander for the two trips to Adelaide.

'Mrs Livesey agreed to pay £500 both to myself and Mr Isaacs in respect of the Adelaide proceedings,' Mr Lander answered, 'and in addition, to pay all travelling expenses and other disbursements incurred on her behalf.'

'But you were unable to practise law in that state,' observed Mr Hunt, for the Official Receiver.

'That is correct,' Mr Lander replied, clearing his throat. 'Two sums of money were paid by Mrs Livesey prior to her leaving by plane for Adelaide on January 9. Mrs Livesey then paid a further £300 on account of travelling expenses and fees for the Adelaide counsel while in the state, as well as £300 to the Child Welfare Department.'

'And how did Mrs Livesey pay for this? From her bank account?' Mr Hunt asked.

'Returning from Adelaide, Mrs Livesey borrowed funds— £500 from Mrs Ruby Johnson, wife of the catering manager of the Australia Hotel, pending receipt of money from England,' Mr Lander replied.

'And is it correct that you organised the mortgage for this to happen?' asked Mr Hunt.

'It is.'

'Did you offer your client counsel regarding these accounts?' Mr Hunt persisted.

Mr Lander said these monies were paid only after Mrs Livesey had been expressly warned and advised against incurring such expenses. 'Prior to her second Adelaide visit,' he stated, 'I again warned Mrs Livesey that the visit of a solicitor and counsel was unnecessary. But she insisted.'

Mr Lander then produced a letter he had expressly given to Mrs Livesey and read part of it out to the court. 'You also stated that you especially desire us both to be present with you in Adelaide when you anticipate being questioned in accordance with information supplied to you and myself by Detective Miller of Sydney CIB, by the Adelaide police, regarding an English matter relating to £27,000.'

Despite the fact that Ethel had not been questioned about this matter in Adelaide, the fear that she could have been, was enough for her to sign and endorse Mr Lander's letter. Messrs Lander and Isaacs's attendance in Adelaide had been justified by their client.

———••———

In the Bankruptcy Court, Justice Clyne had had enough. The list of Mrs Livesey's creditors had blown out even further: there were now several additional creditors in England and the Isle of Man; ten people in Australia who had personally lent Mrs Livesey money; and eleven Australian businesses.

British creditors included the upmarket Liverpool department store G.H. Lee & Co (£100 11s 7d), the exclusive jewellers Finnigans (£190 6s 5d), and Mrs Livesey's Blackpool landlady Margaretta Williams (over £1359). Mrs Williams had in 1942 lent Ethel (who was then Mrs Coradine) a total of £1759 (over $120,000) in cash, mortgaging her own property to do so, on the promise that when Mr Coradine passed away and their house sold, the money would be repaid. When it wasn't, Mrs Williams took her to court and judgment was obtained against Ethel, while she was on the Isle of Man. It was this money that she had used to give Mr Livesey the opinion that she had her own income, so when she had been ordered to repay the funds, she asked her father Frank to help just before she left the Isle of Man. He had managed to pay £400 to Mrs Williams, but £1359 was still outstanding.

The businesses in Australia owed monies ranged from exclusive department store The Myer Emporium to outstanding solicitor accounts with Mac McDonald and Harry Munro, down to accounts not paid to the local pharmacist and newsagents in Edgecliff. And Ethel had managed to repeatedly gain funds from people who had offered help after her failed wedding to Mr Beech, ranging from £700 from Mrs Ruby Johnson, down to poor Mrs Stanbury's savings of £10.

Justice Clyne asked that Mrs Livesey be summoned to appear before his court. He wanted to hear what she had to say for herself.

36

THE CROCODILE-SKIN CASE

On 24 November 1946, the Bankruptcy Court received a medical certificate from a Dr R.N. Reilly in Victoria: an ulcerated hernia incorporating her entire intestine meant Mrs Livesey was unable to travel to the court—but it was certainly noted by Justice Clyne that she had managed to make it across the vast Nullarbor Plain, as far as Melbourne.

Two days later Mr Richardson notified all creditors that they needed to appear before the court with any documents they held concerning their dealings with the bankrupt Mrs Livesey.

James Donohue, who had helped Ethel move back to Sydney's eastern suburbs, was the only creditor to appear on Tuesday, 10 December 1946, with Mr Stanley Theodore Jaques standing in for the Official Receiver Mr Richardson who was on leave.

Mr Donohue was asked about his claim for over £363 ($23,000). He explained that this comprised a £250 loan to

Mrs Livesey, £63 he was owed for six weeks rent at his flat, £24 for rent he paid on a Gowrie Gate flat that he had organised for her, a telephone account for over £11, and £15 for a crocodile-skin leather case.

Mr Jaques noted that Mrs Livesey stated in her affidavit that Mr Donohue had lent £200, not £250.

'At the time I loaned her £250,' explained Mr Donohue, 'she gave me a post-dated cheque for £250, which I have presented to the court, and she told me to present it on 1st February.'

'According to Mrs Livesey, you loaned her £200 and charged her £50 interest,' Jaques asked.

'Not at all!' Mr Donohue replied indignantly. 'I gave her £250—in cash.'

Mr Jaques read further from her affidavit, 'According to Mrs Livesey, there was an arrangement between the two of you that she would not be charged for the rent of the flats?'

Mr Donohue retorted that plenty of witnesses could attest that Mrs Livesey was to repay the rent when her funds came through—including her solicitors, Mrs O'Brien, who was her former landlady at the boarding house in Chester Hill, and Mr Lawson, a boarder at the same address. Mr Donohue replied, 'I understand they also lent her money, though not as much as me.'

Justice Clyne cleared his throat and looked up from his notes. 'How much did they loan the bankrupt?' Justice Clyne intervened, asking Mr Jaques directly.

'Mrs O'Brien had lent Mrs Livesey £150 for a £200 post-dated cheque, and Mr Lawson a further £129 for a £150 cheque, with the difference between the amounts lent and signed for being to cover interest on the loans.'

'I see,' Clyne remarked. 'Proceed.'

'The cheque presented to this court is the only document you have?' Jaques asked Donohue.

'Together with the rental receipt for Gowrie Gate, the telephone bill and the note of promise from Mrs Livesey,' he replied.

'For the gold cigarette case and one ring to hold as security for money lent.'

'That is right,' Donohue replied.

'Do you have any documents to support your claim for £63 for the six-week stay in your flat?' Mr Jaques asked.

'Only the proof that she stayed in the flat,' he replied. 'The caretaker of the building saw her, and her solicitors interviewed her there many times,' adding that a newsreel by Cinesound was also filmed there.

'There is also a claim for £15 for a leather suitcase?' Mr Jaques asked.

'Yes,' replied Mr Donohue with a big sigh. 'Mrs Livesey wanted the case. She told me she'd give me £15 for it, but I refused.' Mrs Livesey had then taken the case when she left, selling it to another creditor for £1. 'She told the girl she had bought the case from me for £15, but did not want it any more!' Mr Donohue stated angrily. 'There are numerous other things she sold and ruined in my apartment which I did not claim for,' he stated in disgust.

The hearing was adjourned soon after Mr Donohue's evidence, and Justice Clyne was starting to get an inkling of how Mrs Livesey operated.

37

MRS LIVESEY EXPLAINS

It wasn't until Tuesday, 4 February 1947, that Ethel finally came before Justice Clyne in the Bankruptcy Court.

The previous Wednesday, 29 January, she had given evidence at the Supreme Court into the investigation of her legal bill to solicitor Mr Lander and barrister Simon Isaacs—in a closed court, much to the press's immense frustration.

Arriving at the Bankruptcy Court with her new legal counsel, Mr Bruce Panton Macfarlan, Ethel caught sight of Ruby and Baydon Johnson talking with another of her hopeful creditors, Mr Grindell. She pulled her shoulders back and walked straight past them with barely a glance.

Everyone stared at her as she entered the courtroom, their eyes curious and hostile, as Ethel made her way to her seat, amid occasional murmurs and snickering from those around her.

She was to be the first witness before Justice Clyne and Mr Richardson; Mac McDonald was representing one of the creditors, Miss Rewa Nicholson.

Mr Macfarlan stood to address the court. 'I should mention to you, in view of the nature of this examination, that the legal expenses in connection with representations by Mrs Livesey at this examination, are being paid by friends in Melbourne and are in no way contributed to by her,' he stated to Justice Clyne.

Justice Clyne nodded, before Ethel was sworn in. The packed court was hushed as her account began.

'Please state your name and address for the record,' Mr Richardson said.

'My full name is Florence Elizabeth Ethel Livesey, and I reside at the Victoria Palace, Melbourne,' she replied clearly.

'How long have you been there?' he asked.

'On and off, for the last few months,' she replied casually.

'Did you disclose in your statement of affairs that you filed in this court all of your assets and liabilities?' he asked.

'Yes.'

'Do you want to correct it in any way?'

'No, I do not think so,' Ethel replied.

'On that statement of affairs, did you show as a creditor Margaretta Williams of number 2 Athlone Avenue, Blackpool, England?'

'No,' she stated.

'In the sum of £1359 9s 3d?' Mr Richardson asked.

'I am not indebted to her,' Ethel replied. On further

questioning she insisted that the matter had been settled through her lawyers there.

'Do you know a sum of £400 was paid off that sum?' Mr Richardson asked, getting her to look back at him.

'Yes.'

'Who paid that sum?'

'I think my father paid that,' she replied. 'He said he would carry on paying it for me.'

'What was the debt for?' he demanded.

'Money lent to my husband,' she stated, 'William Alexander Coradine.'

'Did you sign any documents which would make you liable for this debt?' he asked.

'I cannot remember,' she replied.

Mr Richardson tried not to appear frustrated as he shuffled the papers in front of him and looked up at the large woman before him who had caused them so much trouble over the last few months. 'Are there any other debts you have not shown in your statement of affairs which were incurred in England by yourself?'

'I had accounts before I left, but I left money in England for the accounts to be paid before I left—£600 or something. I left it in my Bank of the Isle of Man account for Nurse Sayle, my father's nurse, to pay on my behalf,' she answered.

'Have you a list of those creditors who were to be paid, or whether or not they were paid by this nurse?' demanded Mr Richardson.

'No,' Ethel replied.

Mr Richardson looked at her for a moment before continuing. 'Did you hold any joint property with your father?'

'No,' she replied.

Mr Richardson handed her a copy of her Isle of Man Bank account. 'Will you look at this document?'

Ethel flicked through the pages quickly and then looked to the Receiver expectantly.

'There was £466 4s in the account on the date you left,' he said.

'Yes,' Ethel said, searching for the date and confirming.

'Not £600,' he remarked.

'I also left some cash with Nurse Sayle,' she answered.

'There are small amounts withdrawn after the date you left England—except for one sum of £210 for Gelling & Cowin.'

'Yes, I cannot think who they are,' Ethel said absently, as if talking about the weather.

'Gelling & Cowin are solicitors?' he suggested.

'I think so,' she replied carefully.

'What was the £210 paid to them for?' he asked.

'I have not the slightest idea,' Ethel remarked. 'It is absolutely news to me.'

Asked if Nurse Sayles had anything to do with the Isle of Man business, Sayles Ltd, Ethel replied that Sayles was a common enough name on the island.

'Sayles Ltd were creditors of yours?' he queried.

'Yes.'

'Did you know that they got a judgment against you?'

'No,' she replied.

'On top of the Sayles Ltd debt, which exhausted the balance

of your account on the 6th of December 1945, did you owe any other creditors other than Mrs Williams?' he persisted.

'I cannot remember, it is a long time ago.'

Mr Richardson looked frustrated; her answers were irritating. 'Give me the names of the bank accounts opened in Australia,' he demanded as steadily as he could.

'The Bank of New South Wales, Adelaide; and the Bank of New South Wales, Sydney,' Ethel stated.

'Have you got the passbooks of those accounts?'

'No, they are at the bank.'

Ethel's lawyer stood and handed Mr Richardson a copy of the Sydney account statement, which he read through.

'This £2000 entry?' he asked.

'The money was sent over by Layton & Co., Lawyers of Liverpool,' she replied, saying it was for part of the sale of a property.

'Who owned the property that was sold?'

'I owned it,' Ethel replied.

'Was it registered in your name?'

'Yes.'

Mr Richardson put the bank statement down in frustration and looked again at his papers. 'Who is Robert Cowell?' he asked suddenly.

'My father's solicitor.'

Mr Richardson told the court he'd received a letter from Mr Cowell, dated 22 August 1946, stating that Ethel's father, Mr Swindells, had confirmed that the £2000 in question was not gifted to him by his daughter, and that it was payment made by Messrs Layton & Co., for the sale of some property in Manchester, owned by Mr Swindells.

'What property is actually referred to there?' he asked her.

'My father had a house at 72 Grove Lane in Hale, Cheshire, and he was very sick,' Ethel replied, adding that her father had given power of attorney to her husband, Thomas Livesey, and wanted the property sold. 'So he gave me a note to give to the bank and get the deeds and take them to Layton & Co. My father being in bed with a stroke, I went over to Liverpool and saw Layton & Co., the cheque was handed to me, and I handed that cheque to Mr Livesey,' Ethel stated, with the most honest look on her face.

Mr Richardson stared at her for a moment. 'What properties did you in fact own, in your own name, at any time?' he asked.

'I had Aigburgh Drive, Livington Drive, Swanston Road, South Wood Drive,' she replied. 'All in Liverpool.'

Ethel then claimed she had no properties in 1943, but in 1944 had two blocks of flats, which were sold at auction, for £6000, she thought.

'Did you get the money?' Mr Richardson asked.

'All but £2000.'

'Who did that go to?'

'My father.'

Mr Richardson shook his head. 'And yet he says he did not receive that amount,' he said. When she did not reply, he asked if those other properties belonged to Thomas Livesey at any time.

'Yes.'

'Did he have them transferred into your name?'

Ethel replied he had, by deed of gift, in 1945.

'This is the flats?' he asked.

'And the houses—two or three houses.'

Mr Richardson nodded; finally it looked like they were getting somewhere. 'You first knew Thomas Livesey in 1943, was it not?'

'Yes.'

'How many houses did you get from him?'

'I am not sure if it was five or six,' Ethel replied, adding that all but two were sold.

'Has Layton & Co accounted for the sale of those houses?'

'Not all to me,' she replied.

'So is money due to your estate from these sales?'

'I left it entirely in the hands of Layton & Co.,' Ethel said, looking suddenly concerned. 'The attorney has to account to me for some more money, has he?' she asked, turning to Justice Clyne. 'If my father says he has not had the £2000, then yes, they will have to account for the £2000.'

'You have two remaining properties in your name?' Mr Richardson asked.

'Yes, two houses; they were withdrawn from sale. I was receiving rent for them—£3 a week from Layton & Co. or some agents from England.'

Mr Richardson was incredulous to learn that Ethel claimed not to know that the two properties were leasehold, and unlikely to be sold at market value until their 75-year leases had expired.

He made his way back to his table and picked up some papers. 'Referring to these proof of debt again,' he began, leafing through the various creditors' claims, 'did you have any prospect of being able to repay that money?'

'Yes,' she replied.

'At the time you borrowed it?' he asked.

'Yes,' she replied, 'from the sale of the properties.'

Mr Richardson suppressed a frustrated sigh. Was the woman as stupid as she was making out? Did she truly not understand that the properties were worth less due to the leases?

'What did you want that money for, the money you borrowed from these creditors?' he asked.

Ethel replied that all her debts were borrowed to pay legal expenses for her Sydney lawyers, Isaacs and Lander.

Mr Richardson changed tack, addressing the £717 6s claimed by Mrs Ruby Johnson, wife of Mr Baydon Johnson, the catering manager at the Australia Hotel, from 1 January 1946 to 3 May 1946. 'What is that for?' he asked Ethel.

'That was £550 borrowed, and that was given to Isaacs and Lander to pay some of their expenses for their presence in Adelaide.'

Mr Richardson then asked if she had any money in her Bank of NSW account in Adelaide in January 1946.

'In Adelaide, no,' she replied.

'Do you know when you exhausted that account?'

'No.'

Mr Richardson was starting to wonder if she really had any business sense at all. 'So in January 1946, you had no ready money at all?'

No, Ethel replied, but before leaving England she had instructed Layton & Co to sell these properties whenever she wanted, and they would be sold at a moment's notice.

Mr Richardson picked up the Bank of NSW account. 'In January 1946 you only had £15 6s in the account?'

'Yes.'

'When you got this money from Mrs Johnson, you had nothing to be able to repay it with?'

'I had the two properties in England—I told them it would be paid with money from England.'

Ethel also confirmed saying the same thing to a Mr Lawton for his £120, and to Mr Baydon Johnson for £217 6s—all, she said, to pay Isaacs and Lander.

Mr Richardson then read out a sum of £70 from Miss Rewa Nicholson, on 19 March 1946. 'Is that an advance?' he asked.

Ethel shook her head slightly. 'I received a letter from my lawyers, from a Miss Nicholson, stating that after all she had read in the paper she would be glad to be some sort of friend, and she would like to give me a trip to New Zealand, and I could live with her sister in Rotorua. She came back to see me after I came back from Adelaide the first time and she said she would like to help me, and she gave me £30. In the letter she told me I could use the money to pay legal expenses or whatever I wanted it for. That £30 was paid in wages and living. Then she said she had a piece of land, and I was in rather a bit of a hole on account of the rent on my flat, and she gave me £40. I received £35 of that money in Munro's office, Harold Munro, solicitor.'

'Do you owe Munro any money?' he asked.

'Yes.'

'How much?'

'I could not tell you, but I know I had no intention of going to Munro at all, it was through Miss Nicholson; when Mr Munro took over I told him I could not pay, and he said that would be alright.'

'You do not show him as a creditor in your statement of affairs?'

'No, and I did not think for what he had done he was going to charge me,' she replied.

Mr Richardson looked down at his list. 'The next creditor is Mr G.E. O'Hagan, husband of your landlady Dorothy O'Hagan, for £200—is that an advance?'

Yes, she replied, for £125, giving Mr O'Hagan a cheque for £200, as he wanted interest on his loan.

'At the time you knew your bank account was exhausted?'

'But I had a cable from Layton saying the property was being put up for sale. I knew I had assets coming here—*they* knew that.'

'Who understood it?'

'*All* the people I gave the cheques to.'

Mr Richardson looked again at his list. 'And there were goods from the Myer Emporium for £21 19s, and Farmer & Co for £55 17s 8d?'

Ethel then explained she was quite solvent at that time, and could have paid those accounts, were it not for Isaacs and Lander, who demanded that she borrow money to pay off their legal bills, otherwise they would drop her case, and all the money she had already paid them would be useless.

Mr Richardson looked down at his list. And so it went: another proven creditor, Civic Hire Services, for £126 18s?

Ethel replied that she had given this sum to Mr Lander to pay the company.

Household Supply, £149 8s 7d, for spirits and liquor? Yes, these Ethel had ordered, but never received, she claimed.

'George Henry Lee & Co., a major department store in Liverpool, for £18 11s 7d, for goods supplied on 11 June 1945 to 6 July 1945?' Ethel claimed no knowledge of these, saying she left England on the boat on 2 July; curiously, she knew these goods were books, even though she stated she had not ordered them.

Lilian Alice Grindell, for £100? Ethel admitted she had given the woman a cheque for £200, post-dated 15 February, 1946. All her cheques were post-dated, she explained. 'I had a cable from Layton to say the money would be there, and then I got a second cable saying the property could not be sold until the middle of February, and I asked them if they could wait until the middle of April.'

'When did you first meet the Grindells?' Mr Richardson asked.

'Up at O'Hagan's, December 1945.'

'What has become of the money you got from Grindells?'

'It has gone to Lander and Isaacs,' Ethel replied, looking exasperated. 'If I had taken Mr Grindell's advice in the first place I would not have been in this position today,' she declared, catching the angry eye of her creditor in the gallery.

'What do you mean by that?' Richardson asked.

'Mr Grindell had repeatedly told me not to keep giving Isaacs and Lander this money. He was in the flat continually when Isaacs and Lander came and asked for money—he kept saying they were getting too much for what they were doing.

I am sorry if I have missed some things out of my statement, but I have been very, very ill.'

'Have you any jewellery or chattels in England?'

'No.'

'You got some jewellery from Finnigans in Manchester?'

'I got a gold set for £180, which I gave to Mr Johnson as security.'

'A silver compact,' Mr Richardson read out. 'Who got that?'

'Mr Livesey got that for his daughter.'

'Three-piece military silver set?'

'Mr Livesey got that—he chose it and bought it himself.'

'A gold half-hunter watch, £48?'

Yes, Ethel replied, she ordered the watch for Mr Livesey; the money came out of her bank account, from properties he originally owned.

Mr Richardson again looked at his list. 'Do you owe Dr Cunningham any money?'

Dr Cunningham said he would never send her the bill, and that he would treat her as a friend, Ethel replied as earnestly as she could.

'Do you owe Robert Cowell, a solicitor in England, any monies?'

No, she replied: any amounts owing were to be paid by Mr Layton.

Mr Richardson looked at her carefully, 'Do you know a Mrs Sarah Stanbury?'

'Yes.'

'Do you owe her any money?'

'Yes, £10.'

'Do you show her debt in your statement?'

'I thought I told Mr Wheatley of Perth, who made out my statement of affairs, of her debt. I had to get out of my sick bed to go down to see him.'

'Are you receiving any money from any source since your bankruptcy?'

'No, only what I have worked for.'

'What about all of these solicitors that you engaged in Adelaide, Melbourne and Western Australia?'

Ethel vehemently explained that she had arrived in Western Australia with just £5, and when she saw the notice of committal against her in the paper, she consulted a solicitor, Mr Wheatley, who said he would help her prepare a statement; in return she would repay him £2 or £3 at a time, whenever she was able. 'In every place I got a position for £2 a week or so,' she said, turning to Justice Clyne, 'but as soon as they knew that I was Mrs Livesey, they told me to pack up and go, and I was put out on the street.'

She said an employment agency in Perth had lent her some money to join her son in Adelaide, who paid off the solicitor's bill at £3 a week. But she couldn't get a job in Adelaide, and instead went to Melbourne, where a solicitor, Mr Barber, offered to help her, saying she could repay him when she was back on her feet.

'Are you working at present?' Justice Clyne asked.

'I am in Melbourne, but I may have lost my job again through coming here. I shall go back to my employment in Melbourne, if I can—I hope it will be there, but of course if they see this in

the paper, I shall be out of work again,' she said. 'I am sick—
I am under a doctor and specialist for cancer.'

'Are you receiving any income from any source whatsoever?'
Mr Richardson asked.

'Only what I earn.'

'Your father is still living?'

'Yes, as far as I know.'

'You are not receiving any money from him?'

'None at all.'

'I have finished with Mrs Livesey, for the present,' Mr Richardson stated, placing his extensive creditors' list on the table.
'But I may get material for further examination from witnesses
who are creditors, who are here in court, and whom I desire
to call.'

Representing his client, Miss Rewa Nicholson, Mac McDonald
stood up to address the court; Ethel's lawyer quickly stood up
as well.

'I shall object to Mr McDonald asking any questions,'
he urged. 'I am instructed that Mr McDonald is acting for
the gentleman who is alleged to have broken a contract of
promise to marry Mrs Livesey, and I do not desire any question
of that kind to be entered into.'

'I think you will find that it is a matter for my discretion,'
Justice Clyne observed.

Mac McDonald looked at Justice Clyne. 'I shall not go into
Mr Beech's matter, I shall be asking questions on behalf of my
client, Miss Nicholson.'

'Then I shall allow Mr McDonald to ask questions,' Justice Clyne remarked.

Ethel bristled visibly as Mac turned towards her.

'You told the court that Miss Nicholson took you to Mr Munro, the solicitor. Is it not the fact that you yourself located Mr Munro?'

'No, Miss Nicholson and I went together to him,' Ethel replied.

'But did not Miss Nicholson, prior to that, come to your flat at Gowrie Gate?'

'Yes, she stayed there on several occasions,' Ethel confirmed.

'And you told her you were pressed for rent?'

'Yes.'

'You got in all £70 from her?' Mac asked.

'Yes,' she replied.

'And none of it was payment for rent?'

'It was not specifically for that.'

'Did you tell her that you had received a telephone message to say that your father was dead?'

'No!'

Mac looked at her a moment with a blank expression. 'Miss Nicholson had told you that she had a block of land in the mountains?' Mac asked.

'She said that she would like to help me further.'

'Did you arrange for her to get a mortgage?' he asked.

'No, she went and arranged it with Mr Munro.'

'Did you offer Miss Nicholson a cheque for £100 to transfer the land to you?' he demanded.

'No, I did not have my cheque book with me.'

'I am suggesting that you offered her a cheque and that you were going to post-date it.'

'I did not.'

'I have no further questions,' Mac said in disgust.

———•+•———

When Ruby Johnson came to the stand, she looked like she was about to cry.

'What is your name?' Mr Richardson asked her kindly.

'Ruby Katherine Johnson,' she replied unsteadily.

'Where do you live?'

'At Caroline Street, Kingsgrove.'

'You have lodged a proof of debt in this estate for £717 6s?'

'Yes, for a loan and to cover my legal fees,' Ruby replied.

'Did you pay the loan to Mrs Livesey?'

'Yes,' she replied, looking over at Ethel.

'In cash?' Mr Richardson asked.

'I paid it to Mr Lander,' she said, turning back to him. 'The sum I loaned was £550, but Mrs Livesey offered me £700 . . . but I did not want to make a claim for £700,' she added hurriedly, 'although my solicitor advised me to—the £17 6s was to pay my solicitor.'

'You advanced her a sum of £550, without any contract as to payment of interest or anything?' Mr Richardson asked.

'That is so,' Ruby replied shakily.

'Did you have any security for your advance?'

No, Ruby replied, but Mrs Livesey gave her husband a gilt set she said was valued at £318. When they realised Mrs Livesey was going bankrupt, they took the gilt set to a valuer, who said it could be bought for £30–40 English money pre-war; they'd since sold it for £50, quickly adding that she would like that credited against her claim.

'It did not turn out as good security as you thought?' asked Mr Richardson.

'No, a lot of things did not turn out that way,' Ruby answered quietly, before attesting that she'd met Mrs Livesey through her husband, who worked at the Hotel Australia.

'Tell me about this conversation asking for money,' Mr Richardson continued. 'What did she say?'

'She asked if she could borrow it.' Ruby looked straight into Ethel's eyes, then quickly turned back to Mr Richardson. 'She told me she had an income of £8000 (over $500,000) a year, or £1500 a quarter—a legacy from her grandmother. She had been spending so lavishly, I believed her.'

Holding back tears, Ruby explained that she had only known Mrs Livesey for a few weeks, but they had become quite friendly, so she lent her the money, and had told her husband she was lending Mrs Livesey the money.

'Did your husband lend her any money prior to that?' enquired Mr Richardson.

Yes, she stammered, tears threatening as she looked desperately towards her husband, who gave her a small smile of reassurance. 'She gave him a post-dated cheque.'

'What did she say she wanted the money for?'

'To pay Mr Lander,' Ruby replied.

'Do you suggest that Mrs Livesey tricked you in any way?' Mr Richardson asked.

'Yes!' she sobbed, tears slowly flowing down her cheeks. She pulled a lace handkerchief from her bag and quickly wiped them away. 'She, she told me she had an income of £8000 a year!'

Sniffling into her handkerchief, Ruby explained that after about a month, when she realised Mrs Livesey had no such income, she rang her to ask when they would get their money back. Mrs Livesey told her she was expecting it any day. 'When I told her I must have it,' Ruby said stifling a sob, 'she became quite abusive. She said "I have enough to worry me without people chasing me for money!"' Ruby stopped, wiping away her tears in annoyance.

'Did she say that to you over the phone?' asked Mr Richardson.

'Over the phone,' Ruby nodded, 'just like that.'

Justice Clyne asked her, 'The post-dated cheque was no good, was it?'

'No,' she replied, looking up at him sadly.

Mr Richardson then asked if Mrs Livesey had mentioned owning any property in England.

'Yes,' Ruby said urgently, 'two houses in England!'

'Did she say what they were worth?'

'Some fabulous amount—she was expecting to get about £8000 for them.'

'Are you sure of that?' Justice Clyne asked.

Ruby nodded furiously. 'Yes, that is what she said.'

———·+·———

William Rignold Grindell was sworn in next, the 45-year-old standing prim before the court.

'What is your occupation?' Mr Richardson enquired.

'I have been on compensation for years—I was crushed in a munition works during the war. My heart is affected and liable to go at any time.'

'Are you a creditor in the estate of Mrs Livesey?'

'Yes, for a small amount,' Mr Grindell replied. 'As well as spending money on her, I put in a claim for £15 that I advanced to her.'

'Was the sum repaid to you?'

'No,' he said, staring at Mrs Livesey.

'Did your wife Lilian Alice Grindell give her any money?'

Yes, he replied, but he didn't know of this until after Mrs Livesey's bankruptcy. 'My wife never told me,' he said. 'Mrs Livesey got it secretly without my knowing.'

He said in return for her £100, Mrs Livesey had given his wife a post-dated cheque for £150, which was now in the possession of the court. 'I knew nothing about the cheque,' he added. 'She got my wife to do everything secretly unbeknown to me, or I certainly wouldn't have allowed her to give it to her without security.'

The Grindells had met Mrs Livesey through boarding-house proprietor Mrs O'Hagan. They had taken pity on her predicament and offered her the best room in their house, where she lived for two or three weeks.

'Your wife was friendly with Mrs Livesey?' asked Mr Richardson.

'Too friendly.'

'As regards your £15 that you advanced to Mrs Livesey, do you think she tricked you into giving it to her?'

'She tricked everybody.'

'Did you regard yourself as being deceived by her?' Mr Richardson asked.

'Yes.'

'In what way?' Justice Clyne interjected.

Mr Grindell said Mrs Livesey had told them she had £5000 coming to the Bank of New South Wales, from England. Mrs Livesey then asked his wife if she could mortgage their home for £500, in return for a cheque for £700. Mr Grindell had told his wife they didn't want £700—only the £500 they'd loaned—and that if Mrs Livesey's bank manager could verify the money was coming, he'd be quite willing to let his wife mortgage the home as security, but only for a short time, as his pension had stopped and their home was all they had in the world.

'Did you attempt to verifiy the funds coming from England?' Justice Clyne asked.

'We made an appointment the next morning,' Mr Grindell replied. 'Our solicitor was to meet us there at the bank, her solicitor Mr Lander was to meet us at her flat.' They waited at the flat for some time, before Mrs Livesey asked if he would run to the chemist and get some aspirin, as she had a headache. As he was leaving the building, a young fellow pushed passed him and headed towards Mrs Livesey's door. Mr Grindell kept walking towards the shops, but feeling a little suspicious, stopped, turned back and knocked on her door. 'The door never opened and I had to force it,' he explained. 'When I got in this young fellow—I found out later it was Mr Lander's brother—had a paper on top of the piano and he was trying to get my wife to sign it. I yelled out, "Don't sign anything until we see the bank manager and our solicitor!" Young Lander said, "What has it got to do with you? This is your wife's property." Well, I told him, I have the deeds and it will take a better man than you to get them from me!'

'Did you verify this £5000?' Mr Richardson asked.

Mr Grindell nodded. 'This was the same morning we had to go to the bank. I said to Mrs Livesey, "Are you prepared to go to the bank? My solicitor is there waiting." She said she could not go—she backed out of it. The young man put on his coat and cleared.' The Grindells then went to the bank, where their solicitor was waiting, and explained that Mrs Livesey had refused to join them. Their solicitor told them it was just as well, as he'd seen the bank manager and advised them to have nothing to do with it. So they didn't mortgage their property—nor did they get any of their money back from Mrs Livesey.

When Mrs Livesey was recalled to the stand after the creditors had given evidence, she stated they were mistaken, or were not telling the truth.

Every time Mr Richardson asked a question, she reputed everything said against her.

Finally, she was allowed to leave the court.

Perhaps not strangely, after that she disappeared again.

38

MRS NAN GLOVER

Two and a half years later, Ethel's name appeared in the papers again. She was living in Brisbane, and the mystery of where she had been hiding out since leaving the Bankruptcy Court began to emerge.

Her notoriety and size had made her easy to pick out in a crowd, and a Brisbane police officer by the name of Voigt had been looking out for her for some time. Like most of the country, he had heard all about the supposed cotton heiress and her guilty conviction on fraud charges dating back to 1933, and he couldn't help but notice similarities with an outstanding case in Brisbane back in early 1935 under the names of Balfour and Grey.

The observant officer took her to the police station for questioning.

'You are Mrs Florence Elizabeth Ethel Livesey?' he asked.

'Yes,' she replied with a sigh. 'Whatever is this about officer? I have a lot to do today and I have only accompanied you here out of the goodness of my heart.'

'You are also known as Florence Elizabeth Ethel Gardiner?'

'Yes,' she replied, 'That was my name a long time ago now.'

'In 1933, to be exact,' he stated. 'And you also used the aliases of Anderson, McEwan, Balfour and Grey?'

Ethel didn't immediately reply, and he thought she was looking at him in a tired but cautious manner. He was onto something, he was sure.

'You resided in Brisbane late 1934 through to January 1935?'

'Yes, I can explain,' she began.

'All in good time, Mrs Gardiner. I have an outstanding warrant for your arrest for passing valueless cheques in January 1935, and obtaining four hats without payment from a milli-nery salon.'

'I had been ill, Inspector,' she began.

'Sub-Inspector,' he corrected.

'Sub-Inspector, and I had absconded from bail in Adelaide before coming to live in Brisbane with a man—a cruel man,' she added. 'All of my offences were brought about by the man I was living with,' she reiterated.

'You admit to these charges Mrs Gardiner?' Voigt asked.

'Yes,' she said.

————

On 12 November 1949, Ethel appeared at the Brisbane Police Court before Mr C.R. Noyes, and again told her story of the cruel man she was living with, who made her commit fraud, all for the sake of her children. This man had told her to cash valueless cheques and give him the money; in return he would get her children out of the welfare home in Adelaide.

She explained to the court the long-term effect the bankruptcy and all the harassment since her highly publicised failed wedding had had on her, emphasising her desire to now lead a quiet life.

She then made one last appeal to stay out of gaol. 'I am earning only £2 a week at present, Your Honour, but if you give me a chance, I will pay the money back.'

Mr Noyes looked at the large middle-aged woman in front of him; her reputation had well and truly preceded her. He took pity, and ordered Mrs Gardiner to make restitution of £5 15s at 5 shillings a week, in default of a month's gaol.

Ethel had escaped gaol this time, but not the notice of the police, the Tasmanian police to be precise.

Three days later, Sub-Inspector Voigt went to see Mrs Gardiner, at her Ann Street residence accompanied by Brisbane Detective Constable Beer.

'I have a provisional warrant for a woman named Mrs Nan Glover, thought to be Mrs Ethel Livesey for having obtained £612 by false pretences at Launceston between February and May 1948 from William Henry Hammersley,' announced Sub-Inspector Voigt, looking up at her. 'Is that you?'

'Yes,' Ethel replied sharply, 'but I never got *anything* like £600 from him.'

Ethel was formally charged at the Brisbane watchhouse at 5 p.m. Soon after 6 p.m., she was taken in a police car to the home of the Government Medical Officer, Dr Cameron, and admitted to the General Hospital.

No application for bail was made three days later, when Mrs Florence Livesey, 52, again appeared in the Brisbane Police Court for extradition to Launceston.

Ethel was made to sit and wait in the lock-up for a week until a policewoman could arrive from Hobart to escort her to her next court appearance.

———

When he met Ethel, Alfred Glover was a 55-year-old widower, farming at Karoola twenty miles north-east of Launceston in Tasmania's north. He had advertised for a housekeeper after the recent death of his wife, and in June 1947 engaged Ethel Nanette Stafford, a stout middle-aged woman who had recently moved from England and was looking for a quiet life. The farm at Karoola certainly provided that. They lived as man and wife for nine months, with Ethel taking on his surname, and she became well known around the small community as Nan Glover.

In February 1948 the new Mrs Glover took a trip to Hobart, the state's capital, and on her return announced to Alfred that she'd like to set up a business—a cake shop. She liked the harbourside suburb Sandy Beach, the tourist centre of the capital, with swimming baths, wooden piers and some of the best hotels in the state, including the prestigious

Wrest Point. She'd found a shop and it was perfect. She told Glover she'd purchase it when funds came through from England, and that when the balance of her funds arrived—£5000 worth—she'd open a joint account in both their names. She then went and leased the shop, Alfred leased out his farm to a neighbour, and they moved south to Hobart.

———

When she was brought back to Tasmania in early December 1949, Mr Glover wasn't much help at her committal proceedings.

'She should go to gaol!' he angrily told the judge. 'That would be her place, instead of running around the country dragging people down to the level of a blackfella, the same as she dragged me!'

The police magistrate, Mr E.G. Butler, fixed bail at £300, with a surety of another £300 for Nan Glover, also known as Mrs Livesey, and committed her to trial for the next sittings of the Criminal Court, on the charge of false pretences on Alfred's cousin, William Henry Hammersley.

No one put up her bail, so Ethel sat in the prison, built by convicts decades before, until her trial nearly two months later.

———

Ethel Livesey was seated alone at the Launceston Criminal Court on Thursday 23 February 1950, before Acting Judge Gibson and an all-male jury. She pleaded not guilty and was not represented by counsel, having deciding to conduct her own defence, openly stating she didn't have the money for a lawyer. She'd certainly seen enough inside courtrooms in her life to know how they operated.

William Hammersley told the court how he had first met Nan Stafford in June 1947 with his cousin, Alfred Glover. Eight months later he was surprised to receive a telegram from his cousin's new wife, asking to meet him at the Criterion Hotel in Launceston on 13 February 1948.

At the meeting she had explained that his cousin had contracted debts before their marriage, and she desperately needed money to pay for them. She could not get her husband to be reasonable, and told Mr Hammersley that she had substantial funds coming from England—more than enough to cover the debt, but that she wanted to pay it off as quickly as possible, before Alfred got into trouble with the law. Mr Hammersley gave her £100 in cash that day.

A week later she met Mr Hammersley again and told him that the £100 had been insufficient and she needed another £50 to cover the old debts, saying she had opened a bank account in the name of Alf and Nan Glover, and deposited £5000 she had received from England into it, but she couldn't access the funds as Alf had confiscated the cheque book. Mr Hammersley handed over another £50.

On 9 March, they met again, Mr Hammersley expecting to be repaid, but his cousin-in-law seemed very distressed. Her father and her brother were arriving shortly from England and she needed money to buy furniture, but still couldn't access the funds from her joint account. Alfred was being unreasonable and she wanted to make her elderly father comfortable when he arrived. Mr Hammersley handed over another £100.

Over successive weeks, she received additional sums of £100, £50 and £150, the latter amount needed to upgrade an electric stove and equipment in her cake shop, which she planned to sell, saying if she couldn't access the joint account, she'd pay Mr Hammersley back with the proceeds.

Mr Hammersley went with his housekeeper, Mrs Rowbotham, to look over the cake business, and said he would take it off her hands for £300, reducing her debt to him down to £250, which she readily agreed to.

Some time later he asked her about the £5000 in her joint account.

Ethel suddenly stood up in court. 'I am sorry, that is a lie!' she interjected. 'I never had a joint account with Mr Glover.'

'Your objection is noted,' the judge said. 'Please carry on, Mr Hammersley.'

Ethel sat back down as the prosecutor continued to ask Mr Hammersley about Mrs Glover.

'She represented herself as a wealthy woman, saying she had £5000 in a joint account, more money in a fixed deposit in Western Australia, and that her father was a well-off retired cotton manufacturer in England, whilst her brother was a wealthy brain specialist—and I believed her,' Mr Hammersley told him.

'Did you ever meet her father and brother?' the prosecutor asked.

'No, they were supposed to be coming to Tasmania and staying at Wrest Point. She told such a believable story, but much later I figured it was fictitious.'

'Have you any idea where the money you say you gave her went to?' Justice Gibson asked.

'No,' he replied. 'She didn't seem to live extravagantly, so far as I could see. She used to fly around in taxis and that sort of thing, but I thought she was wealthy and accustomed to spending money, and that a few hundred were nothing to her.'

'When did you find that the defendant was not married to your cousin?'

'Just after I gave her the last £150—she mentioned that Alfred had cleared out.'

Ethel rose to her feet. 'That is a lie!' she stated. 'I told you on a previous visit that I had a bruised face from falling from a trap. You said it did not look like a fall, and I said "No, Alfred hit me, but I'm not worried as I am not married to him." That was the first time you knew.'

'A definite lie!' Mr Hammersley retorted.

'You will have an opportunity to question the witness shortly,' the judge said to Ethel. 'Please be seated for now.' Ethel sat down reluctantly, with Mr Hammersley openly glaring at her as the prosecutor continued with his questions.

'Did you ever receive any receipts or proof of the money lent?' he asked.

'Of course,' came the reply. 'I had signed, hand-written receipts, but after agreeing to purchasing the cake shop it was down to one receipt, for the £250 still owing.'

'Do you have that receipt?'

'No,' Mr Hammersley said, 'she took it.'

'She took it?'

'Yes, well I gave it to her,' Mr Hammersley explained. 'She asked if she could lend it as her brother was clearing up her affairs, and there were certain notes on it she needed. I gave it to her and did not see it again.'

It was then Ethel's turn to ask some questions. All in the courtroom could see the hatred in Mr Hammersley's eyes as she stood.

'This is an absolute frame-up,' she began. 'As I can prove. Mr Hammersley,' she said, turning to him, 'is it true on one visit I came to you with a bruised face, and I told you Mr Glover had struck me?'

'Yes,' he replied.

'Did I say, I need not stay with him any longer as I am not married to him?'

'No,' he replied. 'You first told me that you were not married when you came and said Glover had cleared out.'

'Were you friendly with Mr Glover?' she asked.

'Yes.'

'Don't you think if I had said what you say, you would have gone to Glover earlier and asked him why he didn't pay his debts?'

'I was very ill at the time and was not able to get about very well,' Mr Hammersley replied.

She looked at him a moment. 'I suggest you never had the receipt you say I gave you.'

'That's a filthy lie!' stormed Mr Hammersley.

'Glover was certainly on your side about the money,' Ethel remarked.

'Yes, he was evidently trying to get it back for me.'

'I would like to refer to the negotiations we had in place with my solicitor, Mr Gee, for repayment of the loan,' Ethel said.

Mr Hammersley snorted, 'You kept me dangling on a string!'

'Mr Gee asked if you would accept £10 a week, and you would not say whether you would do this or go to the police.'

'I finally agreed to accept £10 a week, and the balance when the additional £500 for which you cabled to England, arrived,' he answered.

The foreman of the jury raised his hand, wondering if he could ask Mr Hammersley a question. The judge nodded in agreement and the foreman stood. 'Why didn't you approach your cousin about the old debts?' he asked.

'Alfred was a sick man,' Mr Hammersley replied, 'but I wrote to him three times and never received a reply. He told me later that he never received my letters. I thought at the time that he was trying to avoid me—that he was upset about what had happened and did not want to face me,' he explained. 'Her tale was always so good that I believed her—I even received telegrams supposedly from her brother talking about repaying my loan! I thought the woman was really honest,' he added, 'and that it was only a matter of time before she would pay me. I thought that if I could help her I should.'

'You are not wealthy?' the judge asked.

'I certainly am not,' he replied.

———·—

Alfred Glover was next to take the stand, retelling how he had met Mrs Livesey as Mrs Stafford at her flat in Tamar Street in Launceston, and engaged her as a housekeeper. She moved to his farm at Karoola, and they were never married, even though he let her use his name.

'She told me she was wealthy,' he said to the prosecutor.

'Did you hold a joint bank account with Mrs Livesey?'

'No.'

'Why did you move to Sandy Beach in Hobart?' the prosecutor asked.

'Nan—eh, Mrs Livesey—had bought a cake shop there, but I didn't realise it was with my cousin's money!' Mr Glover replied. 'I thought it was with money from England.'

'Did you put any money into the business?'

'Yes,' Mr Glover replied, '£80.'

'Do you know how much money the business made?'

'No, all I know is I never got any of it.'

Mr Glover first found out Mrs Livesey owed money to his cousin in May 1948, while they were living at Sandy Beach; she asked him to stop Mr Hammersley going to the police, saying she was getting her money from England in October.

'Did she mention amounts?' the prosecutor asked.

Mr Glover nodded. 'Yes, big amounts,' he said. 'I think at one stage I was to benefit by £27,000!'

'How did you find out her real name was Mrs Livesey?'

'She eventually told me, and we parted.'

'Did you see her again?' the prosecutor asked.

'Yes, in Launceston,' Mr Glover replied. 'She sent me an urgent telegram asking to meet—she wanted to marry me!' he said with a sarcastic laugh, sending a nervous titter through the courtroom crowd. 'But I told her, not until she'd paid back Hammersley.'

Next it was Ethel's turn to question him.

'Mr Glover,' she began, 'is it not true you hit me twice while we were together?'

'That's true,' he admitted. 'Once on the chin, and on another occasion I turned you over on my knee and smacked you hard!'

The court erupted into laughter. The thought of the large woman before them being placed over the smaller man's knee was certainly a comical picture to imagine.

'And you got let down lightly!' Mr Glover continued, yelling above the laughter, 'lighter than you let down my pocket!' The laughter started up again, even louder.

'You told me your brother was coming all the way from England,' he stated loudly, trying to talk over the laughter, 'with a power of attorney, and I'd get £27,000, with a possible £50,000 when your father died.'

'That is absolute rubbish!' Ethel scoffed.

'Tell me, Mr Glover,' she started up again as the laughter subsided. 'Is it not true that you had once served a prison sentence for causing grievous bodily harm to two men?'

'You know it's true,' he growled at her.

'And did you not receive £300 from the sale of the Sandy Beach business?' she asked.

'No, it was £250!' he stated, 'to pay back my cousin. And, you were supposed to pay all the accounts, and you left them unpaid and scarpered off to buggery!' The gallery burst into laughter yet again.

'Who paid the butcher?' she demanded.

'Poor little me!' he replied in a high-pitched voice, as once again the crowd erupted.

Ethel turned to the judge amid the laughter. 'Your Honour, the witness is purposely trying to be comical,' she implored.

'I am not!' Mr Glover yelled, to more peels of laughter.

Trying to hide a smile, the judge adjourned the case until the following day, returning Ethel to her cell.

———•••———

On the second day of the case, Ethel called Mr W.M. Deavin, who had leased the Sandy Beach property to her, and solicitor Mr E.A. Gee to testify. Both told the court that she had always been honest and straightforward in the business dealings conducted with them.

When it was time to stand in the dock and give her final address to the jury, Ethel looked sad and resigned. She was about to give the performance of her life, and she threw everything into it.

'Gentlemen,' she began, 'I am perfectly innocent. I admit that I received £350 from Mr Hammersley, but never by false pretences,' she stated in a clear, strong tone. 'And I plan to work, to pay him back.'

She paused for a moment, before continuing. 'As I was working when Mr Glover first met me, I have to ask, how could he or Mr Hammersley ever think me wealthy?' pausing again for effect. 'I have scrubbed and cleaned and, while running the business at Sandy Beach, toiled for 48 hours at a stretch. Would a wealthy woman do that?' she asked, pausing to let them think about it. She had learnt well from her previous lawyers.

'You can see that I did not do the things alleged against me,' she implored. She took a breath and looked her most vulnerable. 'I have been battered from pillar to post these last few years, all because of a splash in the newspapers over a wedding,' she pleaded, fighting back tears.

'Since then, wherever I have gone and obtained a job, I have been turned out, sometimes before breakfast,' she added forlornly, 'after it had been discovered that I was Mrs Livesey.'

She sadly turned to the jury. 'I have nothing now but my two hands,' she implored, holding her upturned hands out towards them. 'And I can only emphasise that I still wish to pay Mr Hammersley, though not all at once, as I will have to work for money,' she stated desperately, needing them to believe in her.

'For four months,' she continued, letting her hands dramatically fall to her side, 'I have been in custody awaiting trial—much of that time ill in bed.'

She stopped and tried to look each juryman in the eye as she continued on. 'I am fighting hard for my freedom, gentlemen.

I ask that you give it to me. Please, in the goodness of your hearts, find me not guilty!'

The jury went out to deliberate at 12.30 p.m. They returned at 2 p.m. with a unanimous verdict: not guilty on all six counts.

'Thank you gentlemen!' Ethel said to the jury as she left the dock, tears flowing down her cheeks. 'Thank you!'

———·—·———

When a reporter from the *Truth* saw Mrs Livesey in the street a few minutes later, her tears had vanished and she showed no signs of remorse or emotion.

'I haven't a shilling in my purse,' she stated, 'and no idea where I will get a bed tonight. But I suppose I'll manage,' she added, looking down the street.

39

MRS ETHEL NELSON

Seven months after she'd been let off in Hobart, Mrs Livesey was back in Adelaide, living in a suburb called Magill, only to be arrested again.

This time Florence Elizabeth Ethel Livesey, 53, domestic, appeared in the Adelaide Police Court for three offences alleged to have been committed by her, four years previous, in 1946.

Mrs Ethel Nelson had obtained a job as a domestic at the home of Jonathan Morris Powell in Lower North Adelaide, from 9 October to 6 November, 1946. His wife was ill and they needed some help around the house, but they soon got more than they bargained for.

On 31 October, Mrs Ethel Nelson had made her way to a second-hand dealer, Rosellen Tredrea, pretending to be a Mrs Ethel Morris living at Fitzroy Terrace in the Adelaide suburb of Prospect, and pawned most of the Powells' good glassware for £2 5s. In early November, armed with crystal-ware and linen, she again returned as Mrs Morris, having moved to Port Elliot, and received a further £4 17s 6d.

Mrs Powell passed away in early November, and Mrs Nelson's services were no longer needed. Not long afterwards, Mr Powell noticed that a few items were missing around the house, but thought perhaps his wife had put them away and he'd find them when he was feeling up to sorting through things. When he recognised Mrs Nelson as Mrs Livesey from the press photos that appeared when the Bankruptcy Court was looking for her, he immediately searched the house for the missing items and, not finding them, reported the theft to the police, as well as the earlier presence of the wanted woman in his home.

Mrs Livesey remained elusive to the South Australian police until November 1950, when one sharp policeman recognised her and promptly arrested her, charging her with the outstanding arrest warrant.

———

On Wednesday 29 November, Mrs Livesey faced court, this time with a lawyer, Mr Philcox, and pleaded not guilty. The charges were read and old Mr Powell slowly made his way to the stand. He told the court about the loss of his property and his wife, while the lady they knew as Mrs Nelson was with them.

The prosecutor next called up the woman from the pawn shop, Mrs Tredrea, who identified Mrs Livesey as the woman who in 1946 had brought in the items she had purchased in good faith—the same items that were later identified as stolen from Mr Powell.

On Mr Philcox's advice, Ethel changed her plea from not guilty to guilty. It was not looking good.

The prosecutor brought Mr Powell back to the stand. With a quavering voice, he added more damning evidence. When his wife had passed away, Mrs Nelson had suggested donating his wife's clothing to the United Nations clothing appeal for people in Europe who were struggling through a tough winter and had suffered greatly during World War II. He told the court how horrified he had been when he noticed a woman wearing his wife's distinct boots a few months later. When he asked her where she'd bought them, she said a woman had been selling off her old clothes; but strangely, the clothing had been a much smaller size than the woman actually selling them. When Mr Powell told her the full story, the woman had insisted on giving the boots back to him. He had sadly thanked the woman, but told her to keep the boots; he was glad they were being used.

Mr Powell told the court how his horror had turned to anger when he knew that Mrs Nelson was really Mrs Livesey.

As Mr Powell resumed his seat, the prosecutor told the court that Mrs Livesey had, since the beginning of 1928, been convicted 26 times—mostly for false pretences—in England, Victoria, New South Wales and South Australia.

Mr Philcox defended his client, saying she'd only had one serious conviction in the past fifteen years, and that she'd had a grim life. She'd had to battle for herself since being deserted in England after marrying at the age of sixteen, and had been left with a small child.

The judge asked Ethel to stand in the dock, and without any qualms sentenced her to two months gaol.

Clasping the dock rail tightly as her sentence was delivered, Ethel broke down sobbing.

———·——

Two months later she was dragged from Adelaide Gaol, back into the Criminal Court yet again, on a charge of having broken her three-year good behaviour bond of £300.

A shattered woman, Ethel admitted she had broken the bond by stealing from the Powells within three years of the bond being imposed.

The court told her son Basil and his wife Sylvia that the full bond of £300 had to be paid. To cover the bond, they would have to sell their newsagency business and residence, which would send them broke and leave them homeless.

Ethel was sent back to gaol to finish her sentence.

Two weeks later, she was released.

And then she disappeared again.

AFTERMATH

In the 1980s, Ethel's estranged son, Frank, went searching for his birth certificate. He could not find it anywhere, and thought momentarily about his mother. If he found her, perhaps she could tell him where he was born.

Ethel was a notorious, selfish con woman, whose choices Frank could never forgive. She was an adventurous woman, an incredibly charming woman when she wanted to be, a woman trying to survive in a man's world, living with her selfish mistakes, of which there were many. He would have known that if Ethel was still alive in the 1980s she'd be old, but perhaps there would still be time.

But where did she go? Did she, upon her release from gaol in 1951, seek work under the name Mrs Livesey? It is doubtful, as that name was forever tarnished.

She was a woman who could not help but spend any money she had, and being middle aged when released from gaol and with limited means to support herself, would more than likely have fallen back into the only means she knew to earn the funds she so desired.

Was she really as sick as she had claimed over the years, and had that illness finally taken her in middle age?

A death notice appeared in the South Autralian *Advertiser,* stating that Mrs Florence Ethel Livesey had passed away in the small country town of Clare, South Australia, in March 1953.

So that was that: Ethel was gone at the age of 55. Or was she?

After ordering the death certificate, it showed the death of an 87-year-old woman who had died from gangrene in her left leg. The details on the death certificate were given by the local undertaker, not a doctor or a family member. Mrs Livesey had died alone.

Strangely enough, there were newspaper reports about a woman looking uncannily like her, eighteen months after she'd been released from Adelaide Gaol. She was being sought for three counts of false pretences in Western Australia. This large, middle-aged woman had a nice little scheme happening, where she'd say she was going to buy a house, then get the keys from the owner or estate agent without even paying a deposit, then show the house to young couples, offering it at a greatly reduced price, and would then pocket their cash deposits before disappearing. Could this have been Ethel? Or was there another con woman of about the same size and age plying her trade against unsuspecting victims?

As to the money—the fortune she came out to Australia with—it looks like she actually spent it. The £40,000 she'd mentioned was perhaps the true value of stock and property she swindled out of her father and Thomas Livesey, but from the bankruptcy files it appears more likely that she received and spent a bit over £27,000 (over $1,400,000) in just over six months when she came back to Australia, on clothes, food, fresh flowers delivered daily, jewellery, travel and lifestyle. She hadn't arrived with that sum; after each asset was sold, she'd get the funds wired into her bank account, and then promptly spend it. The only long-term asset she appeared to have purchased with all that money was her son Basil's newsagency.

About the same time Frank went searching for his birth certificate, he also managed to get back in touch with his brother Basil, after many years. They talked about their families, and their lives, and Frank asked about Ethel. Basil said he hadn't seen her since 1951, and that she was pretty ill at the time. Basil had then lost touch with her, and assumed their mother was dead.

Ethel certainly left a lot of people in her wake.

Her first husband, Alexander Charles Carter, divorced Ethel just after the end of World War I. He died on 17 October 1935 at the age of 43, leaving his considerable wealth of over £4000 to his two sisters, Gladys Carter and Doris Robinson. He is buried at the Southern Cemetery at Chorlton-cum-Hardy in Manchester.

Ethel's first son, Frank Alexander Carter, went to live with his aunt Doris and her husband Stan at their garage in Eccles.

At the outbreak of World War II he signed up and became a captain in the 90 Field Regiment Royal Artillery that landed at Syracuse in Sicily on 13 July 1943. Six days later, at the age of 26, he was killed in action under the shadow of Mt Etna. He left his estate of £544 to his aunt Doris, and is buried at the Catania Commonwealth War Cemetery in Italy.

Corporal Raymond Ward was killed in action in France in 1918. On his military records, Ray Ward's mother was listed as his next of kin, not his wife Ethel.

Jack Smith remains a mystery, with nothing to go on other than his very common English surname—over 2000 English Jack or John Smiths fought in World War I.

Fred Lee and Ernie Stevens are another mystery, both common names at the time, making it difficult to pinpoint them exactly, even though both are listed as co-respondents (persons accused of misconduct with the petitioner's spouse) on the divorce petition of Alexander Charles Carter the younger and Florence Elizabeth Ethel Carter nee Swindells.

In 1937 Ethel divorced William Lloyd Thompson, the man she married when she abandoned her sons Frank and Basil to the orphanage in Cobargo, New South Wales. The divorce went through when she was married to Mr Coradine, so perhaps she was trying to clean up her trail of bigamous marriages—or at least those that she could—before Mr Coradine passed away.

Alfred Spurgess had already obtained a divorce from her in 1928, nearly ten years after their very brief marriage at the end of World War I.

Captain Norman Giblett continued on as the postmaster at Thornleigh in northern Sydney for many years, marrying Ruth Wockner in 1931, nine years after divorcing Ethel.

Captain Midford Stanley Hourn finally got his divorce in 1927, and married Viera McEachern in 1943.

George Addie Anderson, Frank's supposed father, would have been 40 when he married Ethel. Despite Ethel's claims of bigamy, no record of another marriage for George was found, only a record of his death in 1955 in Victoria.

William Coradine died in 1943, and Ethel inherited all his property and belongings, as his legal wife.

Ellen and Leo Kane continued to successfully run the Howstrake Hotel Majestic on the Isle of Man for many years. Ethel's father, Frank Swindells, moved in with them after she left. When he died in December 1947, he left £50 to his nurse, and £100 to his daughter Mabel and her son, together with his late wife's jewellery. The balance of his estate—£205 16s 7p—was left to Ellen Kane. Ethel was written out of his will.

James Rex Beech passed away at the War Veterans Home in Narrabeen, in the hinterland behind Sydney's northern beaches, on 3 August 1965, at the age of 77. He had no next of kin, so the Office of the Public Trustee sent a letter to the Army Service Records asking if he had a will in place when he enlisted. All they could determine was that in 1915 his next of kin was his father—James Beech, Whitby House, Stoke-on-Trent, England.

The Honourable George Roy William 'Mac' McDonald was a Labor Party and then Nationalist politician, and a successful lawyer, before passing away at his home in Bellevue Hill in 1951, aged 68. After his death, his impressive home at 93 Victoria Street was sold to the French Government and became the French Consulate, and was then purchased by British–Australian newspaper heir Lachlan Murdoch in November 2009 for $23 million.

Dr William Cunningham continued practising in Sydney, though he apparently earned a ribbing nickname among his work colleagues of 'Ting-a-ling Cunningham' after the Pekinese pup he gave Mrs Livesey as a wedding gift. Ting-a-ling, the dog, led out his days in the care of May and Mac McDonald.

Messrs Lander & Isaacs paid the Bankruptcy Court £267 15s 6p after their bills of costs were reviewed. Together with recovered jewellery that was sold, the sale of the two remaining English properties, and money collected from Mrs Livesey's bank account, the total sum available to pay the creditors was £429 6s 9p. Though an unproven debt, Justice Clyne and the other creditors agreed to pay Mrs Sarah Stanbury back in full the £10 that she and her husband had saved for their funeral expenses; Mr Stanbury had already passed away by then. Those creditors who at the end of 1948 had maintained contact with the Bankruptcy Court received approximately one shilling for every pound Ethel owed, after legal and court costs were paid.

Thomas Livesey bought back his two properties from Ethel's bankrupt estate for £150, and promptly disappeared off the radar, a darn sight poorer than when he first met the charming Mrs Ethel Coradine!

Ethel's son Basil continued to run his newsagency until he retired; his wife Sylvia, who was liable for the £300 security for Ethel's bond in 1946, renegotiated it with the courts down to £50 in 1951, and they eventually paid it off. She and Basil had two more children and stayed together until Sylvia died from cancer in 1993.

Ethel's son Frank George Anderson was married with five children when he met the love of his life, June Bolan. She was a widow, her husband having died young, leaving her destitute with four small children. Having been put into foster care when he was young, Frank stood by her and they raised the children together, determined not to let their combined brood be torn asunder, and together had another five children, one dying at birth. Frank and June travelled around Australia sundowning for many years. He took on June's surname as well, and became Frank George Bolan. There were too many bad memories with the surname Anderson.

Frank never saw his mother again after 1946.

At the height of her career, if you could call it that, Mrs Livesey was a household name. She had over 40 aliases, eight official marriages, five divorces, four children to different men, and had travelled throughout the Continent, to America, the Orient and the Pacific in the best style possible, had numerous arrests and court appearances, and was imprisoned several times.

Florence Elizabeth Ethel Swindells was an actress, an artist, a stowaway, a spy, a gambler, an air-raid warden, a nurse, an heiress and, above all, a notorious con woman. She could never stay still, she loved a good story, she sought fame and fortune, flaunted the law, deceived and had little regard for others, was impulsive and never seemed to plan ahead.

Ethel was one amazing woman.

AUTHOR'S NOTE AND ACKNOWLEDGMENTS

The Amazing Mrs Livesey is the story of an international confidence trickster working in the early part of the twentieth century. Written as narrative or factional history, real people and actual events have been woven together with fictitious character names, and imagined conversations and actions to bridge occasional gaps in the storyline or account for unnamed people.

When first handed the information on Ethel Livesey, I was not prepared for the astounding number of documents concerning her still held in archives, government departments and libraries around the world, nor where the search would lead. This woman was a treasure trove, and like all good treasures, often carefully hidden. I would frustratingly lose her for a period, only to find her again, often through later criminal cases and mentions of one of her over 40 aliases. She never stayed out of trouble for long.

Con men were relatively common in the first half of the twentieth century, but a female confidence trickster of Ethel's caliber was rare. As well as the scams included in this book, there were at least two other fraudulent crimes reported in the newspapers at the time with a woman using movie star aliases. While these crimes could have been perpetrated by Ethel, I did not include them as I was not sure it was her, even though the timing, descriptions and locations seemed to fit. There is, however, one unverified story I did include, that of Miss Eva Taylor, the fake opera singer and stowaway. I searched in vain for proof that this was indeed Ethel, but with no official charges having been laid, and no photographs or documentation other than newspaper accounts, this was difficult to prove. But as it was such an audacious act befitting her modus operandi at the time, I decided it was too good a story not to include.

Initially I intended to write through the eyes of Ethel's son Frank Bolan, but upon completion of the manuscript I realised the story worked best in the third person. Frank's often-colloquial language has been maintained throughout, giving us a glimpse of the man himself.

As a side note, the currency conversions from the UK and Australian pound to today's Australian dollar equivalents were obtained using an inflation calculator and conversion rates as at November 2015.

———

I could not have pieced together Ethel's story with out the help of an army of people from around the world, who became as enthusiast as I was to find out the truth and helped me pry out all of the facts. A huge thank you to Steve Jackson, librarian and archive assistant on the Isle of Man, the staff at St Luke's Rotorua in New Zealand, the wonderful staff at the British Archives, National Library of Australia, the National Library of New Zealand, State Library of Victoria and State Library of New South Wales, Sean Bridgeman at the National Film & Sound Archive, and Andrew Griffin, Fiona Burns and especially Edmund Rutliedge at the National Archives of Australia. I cannot thank enough those who shared their personal stories about Mrs Livesey and their families, namely Paul Kane, Roy McDonald, Annette Robinson and Sue Monroe. It was a delight to meet you all, and to laugh and share your memories. Annette still has the giant and incredibly heavy white ostrich feather fan Mrs Livesey gave to her as a child; it was a privilege to hold something so extravagant that had been gifted by the woman I had been chasing for so long.

I must thank my wonderful mentor Richard Walsh, who is not only always encouraging and enthusiast, but whose great advice has helped me in countless ways. Thank you R.

Thank you to my brilliant legal eagle and dear friend Peter Gain, for assisting me with court protocol, legal and military jargon. Your response as the first 'outsider' to read the full manuscript was wonderful to receive, and your help, as always, is much appreciated.

I must also thank all of the staff at Allen & Unwin. I once again had the privilege of working with Siobhan Cantrill, as well as Rebecca Kaiser, Katri Hilden and Angela Handley.

Thank you ladies, once again you have polished this gem until it shines.

A huge thank you to Luita Aichinger for telling me what she knew of her paternal grandmother and for handing over her initial research and the precious audiotapes left by her father, and for entrusting me with this story.

And last, but far from least, to my wonderful husband Bert and my long suffering family and friends, thank you all for putting up with me, and the obsession that Ethel became.

Freda Marnie Nicholls